FOX SEA

Guide to

Modern Sea Angling

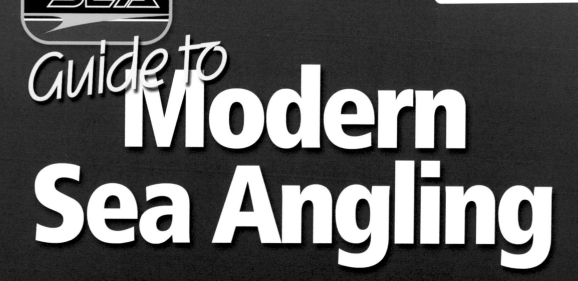

BOAT EDITION

In association with

SeaAngler

THE FOX GUIDE TO MODERN SEA ANGLING - BOAT EDITION

First Published in 2010 by Fox International Group Ltd,
Fowler Road, Hainault Business Park, Hainault, Essex. IG6 3UT.
United Kingdom.

TEL:- +44 (0) 208 559 6500
FAX:- +44 (0) 208 501 1655
E Mail:- info@foxint.com
Web:- www.foxint.com

© Copyright 2010, Fox International Group Ltd.

ISBN: 978-0-9549238-7-7

Designed and produced by Steve Ward Design email:
sward.63@btconnect.com and Fox International.

CONTENTS

The Fox Guide to Beach fishing was so popular the team have decided to do it all again, only this time from a boat. Now this is my sort of fishing, freedom to roam the seas, search out the marks and then send down lures and bait on light tackle to do battle.

Boat fishing has been turned on its head over the last decade and this is down to two things, anglers switching from elastic-like mono to more direct braid, and ditching heavy gear for what I call balanced rods and reels. Braid made it all happen, of course, because now we can fish ultra thin lines in raging tides using minimum lead weight. This means when we play a fish we are not playing the sinker, which happened in the not so 'good old days'.

The new ultra thin lines allow the fish to come alive and any angler that's downsized his gear to fish this way gets fantastic fishing. I tell you, catch a 10lb bass on lure or live bait on a 12lb class rod and reel and you are going to have the time of your life.

And this is what this book is all about - having the time of your life. Boat fishing isn't getting harder - know where to fish and you are going to get your braid tugged really hard.

So with author, Alan Yates' help, stop read, learn and listen, then put into practice what he advises. But I hear you say, hang on, Alan is a shore and specialist match angler. He is but he does have a lighter side; he loves boat fishing too.

I reckon he's had more 10lb bass than you afloat and if you ever meet him in a bar ask him to tell you about the 200lb common skate he caught off the Irish coast on a flimsy outfit. Bet you buy him a pint afterwards!

Alan logically touches on all the subjects that make a successful boat angler; tackle, tactics and methods, the species you are likely to catch and the baits and lures that take fish.

He also covers the areas of charter fishing, angling from small-boats, competition fishing afloat (well that's a surprise!) and how wind and weather especially affects boat fishing. And on those days when it's blowing a hoolie outside, you can sit back with this book, read and learn and dream about the days when the weather breaks and you can get afloat.

Mel Russ, Editor,
Sea Angler magazine.

As a lifelong sea angler I have majored on shore fishing, so getting afloat in a boat is still something of a treat for me and that's why I feel especially qualified to write this book – I am not a boat fanatic, but I was raised among the dinghy fraternity and have fished afloat on all types of craft all around the UK, Ireland and the rest of the world. Destinations include America, Africa and fish-stacked Iceland and Norway.

For many boat anglers, myself included, going out in a boat is not always straightforward. There is the small problem of the green lean (seasickness), while the fear of being afloat in a small craft can put some people off the idea. Not everyone gets sick or anxious, and hardened boat anglers might not consider it a problem. However, for the average angler it is a consideration that gives boat angling a hard edge.

The threat of danger, or putting your life in peril, is something many anglers cannot dismiss easily and it overshadows the positives of boat angling. The problem has been magnified in modern times because increasingly the inshore waters have been fished out, so reaching the bigger fish is very often only possible aboard the long-range charter vessels. A trip involves several hours' steaming time – not every boat angler's ideal trip, because invariably you encounter rougher seas.

My advice to anglers who are nervous about boats is to go with your gut instinct. It's a bit like sitting in with another driver in his car – if you feel uneasy, don't go. This is why many anglers have opted to buy their own boat.

Having said that, most modern day charter skippers are totally professional. Nowadays there are so many regulations from the Department of Trade and Industry that charter boats are far safer and skippers more safety-conscious than ever before. Most modern charter fleets are far more angler-friendly than in the past, when anglers were barred from the cabin or the skipper sat reading the paper all day long and let them get on with it.

You are, though, still dependent on the boat handling and fish location skills of your skipper, and that is why many anglers love – or hate – charter boat fishing. You can catch lots of fish on a boat, even with limited skill, although many want to have more influence over their success than a charter can provide. This is another reason why owning your own boat is so popular – it gives you choice and flexibility.

This book is aimed at giving both types of boat fishing an airing, as well as all the latest tackle and techniques, and no matter what type of boat fishing you prefer it is dealt with in the following pages. If you are considering trying boat fishing for the first time I hope the following advice and information will help you enjoy being afloat.

Finally – before we launch, please consider your safety carefully. You can fall overboard from a dinghy, charter boat or the mooring pontoon and none of these is the place for the careless or the fearless, so take care. The decision to go afloat in the first place is always yours, remember that!

Alan Yates

Chapter 1

Modern Tackle

Chapter 1 Modern Tackle *Rods*

The variety of rods for boat angling is huge, with the experience of a hundred years and more having gone into their design and development. Modern materials like carbon fibre and more recently some of the space-age fibres like Kevlar have had a revolutionary influence, allowing the production of stronger and lighter rods. There is virtually a rod for every taste, ranging from the stiffer more powerful blanks for the largest species to the latest whip-thin wands designed for use with micro braid lines. Most anglers have their own preferences for rods, which is why the variety in designs is so wide. Here we are going to deal with the basic favourites designed for tactics most used in the UK and Northern Europe.

A rod for boat fishing must not be too long, so that it can be handled comfortably in a limited space. Obviously the larger and more roomy the boat, the more scope for longer rods. For instance, on the Continent large party boats for uptiding are common, and these craft allow more or less beachcaster length rods to be used. In the UK most boat rods are usually under 10ft, with the longer ones designed for uptiding, which we shall deal with later. Shorter rods are preferred for downtiding, while for the large species such as shark and conger shorter, stiffer and more powerful rods are the essential weapons.

Below: Two different casting weight tips cover the casting options of 6oz or 8oz leads.

and the line runs below the rod. Fewer rings are then required to ensure the line follows the curve of the rod.

The stiffness and power or strength of a rod is given by its class or line rating. This figure is quoted on the rod in Imperial lbs and nowadays more often in metric kgs and originally came from the International Game Fish Association's (IGFA) line breaking strain rating. This basically is the breaking strain of the line best suited to the rod so that it is flexed to the maximum when the quoted line nears its breaking strain. This ensures the rod will withstand the hardest lunges of a hooked fish, providing the reel's slipping clutch or drag is set properly and the angler shows a degree of skill. Many differences exist between manufacturers' and angler's interpretations of class and

> *"The bend of the rod cushions the lunges of the fish allowing the angler to put pressure on the fish with less risk of breaking the line or pulling the hook out."*

line ratings, but fortunately wide range of line sizes will work efficiently over a range of rods. However, the class ratings are a handy basic guide to help the angler put together a collection of suitable rods to cover the aspects of the sport he favours.

In general the rating system is based around monofilament lines, which have a large degree of stretch – unlike modern braid lines which lack any stretch at all. This has meant that anglers now tend to err on the lighter side in terms of line ratings when choosing rods for braid, and in most cases rods have become slimmer and more supple than in the past. This is especially so in the rating class between 6lb and 30lb, where braid lines are often favoured. Above that rating a rod needs to be stiffer to physically lift very large fish through the water column.

A rod is essentially a means of cushioning the lunges of a fish which would otherwise break the line. It also allows the angler to keep the line away from the boat. Rod length is often an individual choice, but it must stay within certain parameters to make it easy to handle.

Most of the rods produced for the UK boat angling market are for use with multiplier reels, although the fixed-spool reel is gaining in popularity, so the first consideration when selecting a rod is the reel it is designed for. Because a multiplier reel is positioned on the top of the rod, facing upwards, more rings are required, especially at the tip end to keep the line from crossing the rod between rings when it is curved and under tension. Rods for fixed-spool reels have fewer rings because the reel is slung under the rod

Downtide boat rods are generally between 6ft and 8ft long and are designed to fish tackle downtide from an anchored boat. Any longer and they are cumbersome in a limited space, especially on board a crowded charter boat or a small dinghy.

"A 50lb class rod in action fighting a shark. Note that the rings are spaced so they keep the line off the blank when the rod is bent under pressure."

Downtide rods are available in a fairly wide variety of line/class ratings: 5lb-10lb; 10lb-15lb; 15lb-20lb; 20lb-30lb; 30lb-50lb; 50lb-80lb.

There are other spans of line ratings, and it is common for some of the models (multi-rated) to cover a wider range of line strengths in an effort to make them suitable for the widest possible variety of fishing methods.

A 10/15lb class rod in action in the calm of a Norwegian fjord.

A single rod will never be suitable for all types of fishing, each rating being designed and suitable for a specific range of lines and, in many cases, species or methods. Rods may be designed for very light mono lines, or braid lines for general bottom fishing and light wrecking, up to the heavier lines required for wrecking and for serious big fish like conger, shark, common skate and overseas for big game. However, the latest multi-tip rods are more versatile, with three tips each of a different line class.

The 5lb/10lb/15lb/20lb/30lb class ratings are most often chosen for UK boat fishing, with the lighter end ratings suitable for drifting with a baited spoon in the estuary, or the use of micro braids. Other ratings up to the 30lb class are ideal for general bottom fishing or light to medium wrecking. Not all anglers will choose the same rod for a specific task, and the lightness of the rating is a personal choice, often linked to the angler's view of his own skill and the enjoyment level he requires.

Individual angling skill will affect how you handle a rod, and this is where the choice is directed. Many anglers in modern times prefer to fish lighter, far lighter than the old standards and with a degree of skill this is highly feasible, practical and enjoyable.

Let's look more closely at the line class categories and give a few examples of the likely type of fishing they may be chosen for. Remember, the line class is accepted as the line that will fully bend the rod before the line breaks, thus cushioning it from the lunges of a large fish. There is a degree of overlap in line breaking strains that can be used with a specific rating.

6lb-10lb The lightest rods in this class are ideal for use with the lowest diameter micro braid lines for fishing sheltered shallow estuaries with a baited spoon for flatfish, or simply testing your skill in calmer conditions. This is a superb rating for fishing for black bream with light mono over a calm summer reef. The higher end of the range offers that bit more power and a challenge for those who like fishing light with a live sandeel for bass, really light fishing with a single lure over a wreck, or inshore trolling for bass.

10lb-15lb Lots of boat anglers now prefer a 10lb/15lb class outfit for the calm, quiet days when fishing with light gear can be more fun. This class is also the ideal average for use with braid line. It is also suitable for light wrecking, or fishing for bass or pollack with a live sandeel, a jellyworm or a similar lure.

15lb-20lb An all-round favourite rating for the inshore dinghy angler or for braid fishing over wrecks with live sandeel or lures like the deadly shads and jellyworms, which come in a wide range of sizes.

20lb-30lb This is the most often chosen class for the charter boat angler using mono or braid lines because it covers so many options and is powerful enough to handle the larger leads sometimes required with mono. This is considered the all-round class, light and supple enough to offer enjoyment when lure fishing yet strong enough to fish a wreck with a pirk and lures. If you can only afford one boat rod, or want a model to start out with, this is it.

30lb-50lb Here we have the heaviest rating for use with large 300g-plus pirks fished over a wreck using strings of Hokkai feathers or lures where multiple catches of cod or pollack need pumping to the surface. This is the rating required for deep water wrecking at anchor, and baiting with large whole mackerel flappers for conger or ling. It is also an ideal choice for the more sporting shark fishing in the UK for porbeagles and blues.

Shorter down tide rods are sometimes called stand up sticks for fighting fish standing up.

50lb-plus This class is becoming redundant in the UK with the popularity of braid line, although it is what is required for bullying a record conger from the wrecks or shark fishing. Generally, heavy class rods of 80lb and upwards are reserved for tropical game fish like marlin and tuna, or the largest shark species.

"Uptiding is a favourite method for catching smoothhound like this double figure fish that fell to the author."

Uptiding, or boat casting, became popular in the 1970s and owes much of its original development to Essex skippers Bob Cox and John Rawle. The technique requires a slightly longer rod, usually between 8ft and 10ft, to enable the boat angler to cast uptide or away from the boat. The theory is that there is less disturbance and noise away from the boat's hull, while in practice the method offers the option of covering a wider area of the sea bed and avoiding the tangles caused by downtiding, when all rigs are swept to the same line down the stern of the boat.

Above: Cast from a boat with care.

Uptide rods are based on the same design principles as beachcasters, although they are mini versions and in the UK mostly for the multiplier reel.

Uptide rods are not classed by the line class rating, but rather by the lead weight they are suitable to cast. This runs from 4oz up to 10oz, with several models having a crossover between the weight range – i.e. 4oz-5oz; 5oz-6oz; 6oz-8oz; and 8oz-10oz. This allows anglers to choose a rod(s) suitable for the fishing encountered, bearing in mind the species, strength of tide, depth of water and type of boat. The latest uptide models offer multi-tips, rated to cast between 2oz-6oz and 6oz-8oz.

The multiplier reel is favoured for uptiding in the UK, so most rods for this job are fitted with rings specifically spaced for the multiplier reel (more on ring spacings and type later). This is because the multiplier has always been favoured for all types of UK shore fishing, fixed-spools being seen as cumbersome and for beginners.

However, on the Continent the fixed-spool reel is preferred for uptiding, especially from the larger charter boats, because it allows the use of lighter lines. Modern-fixed spools are very well balanced and, unlike the models of the past, have more cranking power. Their biggest advantage is that the open spool flow allows a heavier lead to sink quicker, and this can be crucial when casting uptide in a strong rip. So don't dismiss a fixed-spool for uptiding – like some other methods from the Continent it is being adopted in the UK.

"A heavy lead sinks quicker and 8oz is often more suitable for uptiding in very strong tide."

The most recent features introduced to boat rods, especially uptiders, is a twist and push-in butt. This allows the rod to be extended for casting and then pushed back inside the butt to allow more room when fishing. Adjustable screw reel seats are also more widely available – these allow the reel position to be altered to suit the angler's casting style and while fishing according to the room in the boat.

Uptide rods are also increasingly used by some charter parties on the larger boats for wreck lure fishing because of their extra length.

BRAID RODS

Rods designed for use with braided line generally have a more through action and are softer than those for use with monofilament, simply because braid has zero stretch and a stiff rod will not only exert more pressure on the hook hold and any knots, but could also break the main line or hook snoods. Braid rods are slimmer and of a softer build, with a through action to cushion the most powerful lunges of the fish. More rings are therefore required to allow the line to follow the bend of the rod and not cross the blank between rings.

In recent years the low profile hard loy lined rings have been favourite among manufacturers of the best of these rods, with low rider ring design completing the slimline package. Most specialist braid rods are produced within the 5lb-30lb class, and an increasing number come with a range of two or three separate tip sections. These are ideal for the angler who wants one rod for several tasks, especially when using braid.

Braid can be hard on rings, so quality products like those from Fuji or Seymo are more or less standard.

It is possible to use any rod with monofilament or braid line, although the action of the rod will affect the hook hold. To get around the problem of a stiffer rod, a mono shockleader can produce a cushioning effect when using braid main line.

STAND-UP RODS

Stand up rods, also called stand up sticks, are generally shorter, stiffer rods of 6ft to 7ft designed for heavy wrecking or the larger species like shark, conger and big game – their stiffness being required to lift the largest species up though the water column. Short stiff rods can handle a multitude of boat angling tasks when using mono and that was the old

Most UK anglers prefer the stand up rod style for medium sized fish

style, especially for wreck fishing when heavy pirks and big fish were being hauled from the depths. Softer rods have become more popular as this style of fishing falls from favour.

PIRK RODS

In recent times rod design has expanded to cover a wider range of fishing tactics and techniques, and the pirk rod (rated 30lb-45lb) is one that has been customised for the specific job of fishing large metal 'pirk' lures in conjunction with one or more large feathers, lures like Hokkais, shads and the Norwegian favourite 'Gummi Makks'

over deep water wrecks and in the fish-packed waters of Norway and Iceland.

Anglers started using uptide rods because their extra length and softer action improved the sporting side of the style with both single lures and pirks. That led to the manufacture of a rod specifically for fishing with pirks. This is a specialist tool built to handle heavy 500g-plus pirks with lures, and to pump large fish from deep water as in the Norwegian fjords or some deep water UK wrecks. Whilst fishing with a lighter blank for the larger species can be more enjoyable, with a single lure catching a single fish, the method of fishing a pirk with two or three large lures on a paternoster above it is only practical with a stronger, stiffer blank.

QUIVER TIP RODS

Modern boat match rods have adopted quiver tips since the increase in the use of braided line, which greatly enhances bite indication. Rods with a range of different diameter tip sections, often fibreglass tips on carbon rods, offer improved bite detection in different tidal, line and lead combinations. Designs include bass rods for fishing live sandeels or mackerel with a range of tips to suit the lead required to fish in a specific tide strength. The lightest of these includes the Mediterranean designs for match fishing with ultra-light tips and low diameter mono or micro braid.

Above: Multi tip rods are increasingly popular to allow the angler to cover several tide and lead options.

"A tidy, well-equipped charter boat is always a sure sign of a top skipper."

"Modern line guides are the low profile design and they are used on many of the latest low diameter rods giving them a smoother and less cumbersome action and feel."

A high build epoxy resin finish is standard on intermediate rod ring whipping making them tough and very resistant to corrosion.

The quality of a rod's fittings usually dictate its staying power so looks for good quality rod rings, whippings, reel seat and a comfortable handle.

ROD RINGS

Rod rings or line guides need to be of sufficient number to guide the line along the rod so that it follows the curve of the blank when it is bending without touching or crossing it. The softer the rod and the more it bends, the more rings it requires. There is also a difference between the ringing of rods for multiplier and fixed-spool reels. A fixed-spool reel is slung underneath the rod so fewer rings are required to guide the line evenly along its length. A multiplier faces upwards, and it is here, with the line running along the top of the rod, that ring numbers and spacing are more crucial.

Line guides have advanced enormously in recent years with the introduction of smooth material inserts of silicon carbide, ceramic and aluminium oxide.

These not only extend the life of the rings, but the line that runs through them.

Light, low-profile line guides are preferred for the slimmer rods so as not to ruin their balance and action of the rod. Many such rods designed for braid feature hard wearing, single-leg lined rings. For the more powerful rods, guides tend to be sturdier and heavier. In all cases the number and size of the guides should not destroy the action of the blank.

Quality lined rings are essential, and most of those from the major firms are extremely tough – however, economy rods often feature inferior rings as a way of reducing costs.

Tip rings are subject to major wear, and lots of anglers replace lined tip rings with a single piece stainless steel tip ring (Diamite) which is far more hard-wearing.

ROLLER RINGS

Roller rings were first employed on rods for use with very heavy or even wire lines. In modern times these rings have been greatly improved, so that now many downtide rods above the 30lb class have a roller tip ring fitted as standard. This eases the pressure on the ring and allows the line to flow smoothly through it. The more powerful rods in the 50lb-plus class,

A roller tip ring.

and those for big game fishing, often feature roller rings throughout, although recently the popularity of braid has seen fewer anglers use wire line for deep water UK fishing – which does require a rod with roller rings. The best of these rings come from AFTCO.

WHIPPING

Rod rings are secured to the rod blank by means of whipping silk which is laid along each of the rings' feet. Some manufacturers are starting to secure rings with a wrap of carbon fibre, which is tough and looks good – until you need to replace the ring. Normal silk whippings are coated in a tough epoxy resin finish with several layers (high build) built up to add extra protection.

Double whipping is common on the heavier rods to add extra security to rings, while fancy whipping patterns are a cosmetic feature of many of the more expensive game rods.

REEL SEATS

Tubular fixed reel seats are essential for boat fishing rods because a powerful fish can easily dislodge a weak or temporary fitting. Most rods feature metal fixed tubular reel seats with two screw down locking rings, although adjustable reel seats have been perfected and are increasingly available on many models. A point to consider when buying a rod is to ensure that the locking screws of the reel seat do not hamper your grip of the rod. Most anglers hold the rod just above the reel seat so that they can support the reel's side plate with their palm, so look out for a reel seat with the screw below it. A screw on the top side of the reel seat provides a less effective and colder grip, especially during the winter or if the fishing is hectic.

HAND GRIPS

Modern rod hand grips are mostly of foam EVA which provides a good dry grip in all weathers because water is expelled rather than soaked up. You particularly need a grip the length of your hand above the reel seat so that your hand and palm can support the

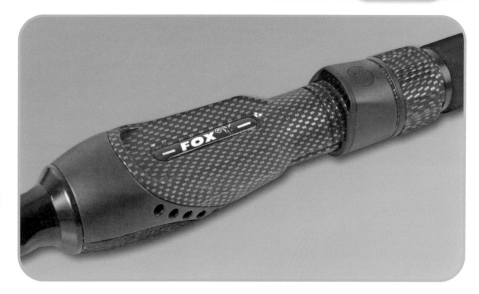

A fixed reel seat is standard on most boat rods.

reel to prevent it rocking about during the retrieve. There are still a few manufacturers who use cork, and this is a stylish addition to the more expensive rods, although not so efficient and easy to keep clean as the modern materials.

BUTT GIMBAL

Boat rods of 30lb class and above often feature a butt gimbal. This is a slotted metal end to the butt, used to connect the rod to a waist belt butt pad for more control of large fish. For big game a harness is also used to support the reel (more on this later).

A rubber butt cap is standard on most rods, and this prevents wear to the bottom of the rod and the deck of the boat. Most rods with a butt gimbal also have a rubber butt cap which can be removed when the gimbal is required.

The butt gimbal and butt cap.

A huge range of tackle is available for the UK boat angler from a wide range of manufacturers. Within the choice there are varied designs from the UK, Europe and increasingly the World. Price always reflects quality and if you buy cheap gear it will let you down so always buy the best you can afford and of a recognised make. One rod and reel is never enough and many anglers find that a range of rods and reels are essential to cope with the various methods, species and venues.

Multiplier reels are used almost exclusively by UK boat anglers, and they have been refined over recent years to include ball-bearing races, making them ultra smooth running. Improvements in gearing, balance, the drag systems and retrieve ratio have made the multiplier by far the best reel for downtide, uptide and wreck fishing around the world, especially when there is a need for fish to be winched up from the sea bed.

While fixed-spools are popular throughout Europe, especially for uptiding, their reputation of being enlarged freshwater reels with a poor ability to crank up heavy weights remains, despite modern versions being far superior to those of a decade ago. Fixed-spools are still a rare sight on a UK.

Multipliers come in a range of sizes and weights – like rods they are rated for use with a capacity of a particular line diameter, although most manufacturers follow a standard reel size based on the original Abu Garcia rating, starting with the smallest reel for boat fishing, the 5000, and going up to the 9000. Above that size the Penn system (1/0, 2/0, 3/0 upwards) is commonly used by manufacturers, so look for 10, 15, 20, 25 or 30 in the reel's model number. Other manufacturers use their own set of numbers, so take care that you check the reel's line capacity, especially if buying unseen on the Internet.

The size of a multiplier is most important in terms of its line capacity and the diameter of line it is designed to hold. A giant reel with a low diameter line and the spool only partially filled would take ages to retrieve, while a small reel with a heavy line would fill up quickly and not hold enough line. Choosing the correct reel size for the length and diameter of line required for the fishing you are doing is of huge importance, and this is why one reel is not able to handle all fishing situations.

For inshore dinghy fishing in shallow water a reel holding 250 yards of 20lb mono is adequate. Use micro braid line with a finer diameter and an even smaller capacity reel will cope. Afloat in the ocean in search of big game, the line capacity may be talked about in terms of 1000 yards and 100lb breaking strain, so a really large and heavy reel is required. Between those two extremes are a host of reel sizes, each suited to a particular venue, species and/or fishing situation.

Multipliers get their name because each turn of the handle multiplies the number of turns of the spool via a set of gears. It is important to use this gear ratio to your advantage because it obviously affects the retrieve rate,

The multiplier is the most popular reel for boat angling and there is a choice of designs and sizes to suit the variety of boat angling tactics and methods.

MULTIPLIER MODELS

5000 and 6000
The smallest multipliers are mostly associated with shore fishing, but their capacity (250 yards of 15lb/ 250 of 20lb line) is suitable for inshore dinghy fishing and they are being used increasingly with the low diameter micro braids. The tougher, more expensive models are best.

7000-9000
This is the most popular choice for all-round boat fishing, especially inshore or light wrecking. There is a large selection of makes and models, including those with lever drags. Line capacity is usually around 250 yards of 20lb, and the retrieve ratio 4 to 1 up to 6 to 1.

1/0, 2/0 and 3/0
These are the heaviest of the models used for UK boat fishing, mainly wreck fishing, with a capacity of 350 yards of 30lb line, a 4 to 1 ratio, a one-piece frame and spool for extra strength, and a lever drag.

4/0-12/0
The largest of the multipliers, these are used for heavy wrecking up to big game.

and therefore the time it takes to reel tackle or fish up in deep water, or the speed of a lure. A few anglers may prefer a single reel for all their fishing, but most realise that the line capacity, gear ratio and cranking power are the most important considerations when choosing a model. Fishing a deep wreck with a reel that only retrieves three turns of the spool to one turn of

the handle, it will take an age to retrieve and so a larger retrieve ratio (5 to 1 or 6 to 1) is essential.

Line diameter also has an effect on the retrieve ratio, simply because thick line will fill the spool quicker, therefore increasing the length of line per turn of the handle as the spool fills. Some multipliers offer dual retrieve ratios,

with a reduction occurring in the gear ratio when the spool is put under a set amount of pressure when a fish is hooked. This prevents the hook being pulled from the fish's mouth, but also allows a more speedy retrieve when the rig is fishless. Motor drive reels are also increasingly common, and have some merit in really deep water or for the less able angler.

FREE SPOOL

There are several types of free spool releases, usually situated on the handle side of the reel. The lever is the most positive, robust and reliable, although lots of the smaller modern multipliers have an automatic press button free spool release which is automatically returned into the drive position when the reel handle is turned. The button type does tend to allow water into the workings of the reel. The third system is via a lever which also operates the drag system, and these are becoming increasingly more sophisticated and popular.

LEVER DRAG

Many boat anglers prefer the lever drag system to the old star drag, although the latter has been refined in recent years. The more expensive reel models have a smooth, firm lever system which does not jam or lock up like some star drags

do. Most lever drags include a pre-set which allows the user to set the reel so that the pressure on the line releases the drag to prevent line breakage. When landing a large fish the drag can be tightened by over-riding this pre-set. Lever drag reels do not like being totally immersed and that is a point to be aware of, especially with some of the cheaper models, because if the drag washers and plates get wet they clog, oil and grease soak the washers and allow the drag to slip, and over time salt water in the drag can also cause the drag and lever to lock up.

STAR DRAG

Most basic multipliers have a star drag, a slipping clutch which allows the spool tension to be set via the star so that a diving fish cannot break the line. Recently these have been greatly improved by a flat or rounded section on the ends of the stars for easier

adjustment and a click system that allows more accurate setting and prevents the drag locking up when it is tightened down. More expensive models tend to have a pre-set which prevents the drag becoming locked down – the clutch slips under a predetermined tension, and once this happens the drag can be adjusted to suit the situation.

Setting the drag:
Set the star drag so that it allows the spool to slip and release line just before the maximum rod curve is reached. This needs to be done with line through the rings and the rod bent to produce the maximum pressure – just pulling the line off the spool does not take into account line friction against the rings and the pressure of the water. In general the setting is 25% of the line's breaking strain, but you will find that lever drags can be set more accurately than star

A lever drag allows instant adjustment of the drag and many models have a pre-set mechanism.

drags, the cheapest of which lack the click setting and are even less adjustable.

MAGNETIC BRAKES

A few of the latest multiplier boat reels have magnetic casting controls built in for heavy shore fishing or uptiding, but they are particularly useful for novices, who otherwise tend to experience overruns when dropping tackle to the sea bed. Casting uptide is improved with a magnetic reel simply because it reduces the chance of an overrun. The magnets are adjustable – the closer they are to the spool, the more they slow it down.

LEVEL LINE

Some multiplier reels have a built-in level line device, a small cage through which the line is threaded. It runs back and forth over the front of the spool to help lay the line neatly on the reel. In my opinion the level line is more trouble than it is worth, especially for the novice, because when an overrun occurs as tackle is dropped too fast to the sea bed it can make unravelling it very difficult. With practice it is easy to learn to support the reel with the palm of your hand and lay the line on the spool with your thumb. Don't be suckered into buying a multiplier with a level line, because in the long term it will cause you more problems than it will solve.

RATCHET OR LINE OUT ALARM

This useful device signals a bite as the line is pulled from the spool. On many multipliers the free spool in ratchet mode is easily pulled out by the tide, so the drag system is used to tighten the spool so that it holds. A bite, though, can still pull out line and signal the presence of a fish on the ratchet. The ratchet is also a handy device when threading line through the rod rings as you set up. Left in free spool, overruns are more likely.

ANTI REVERSE AND DUAL SPEED

All good multipliers have an anti reverse

The star drag is situated under the handle. The more expensive models like this Shimano have a smooth drag system that will not lock up.

Above: This angler is wearing a rod harness that clips to the reel for added purchase and comfort.

Left: This reel has a built-in depth counter.

which prevents the handle rotating as the line runs out, a problem with old style reels that resulted in rapped knuckles. Dual speed reels are increasingly common, especially for deep water or game fishing where a faster retrieve may be required when a fish is running towards the boat or when tackle needs to be brought up from deep water. In some cases the second gear clicks in automatically as tension on the spool lessens: on others a small lever at the side plate is clicked over to increase or reduce the retrieve ratio.

LINE COUNTER

Some of the larger wrecking reels incorporate a built-in electronic line counter which allows the angler to fish the bait or lure at a precise depth. Catch a fish and you can mark the depth for the next drop. Such counters are an invaluable aid when fishing pirks in very deep water such as the Norwegian fjords.

REEL HARNESS

Fixing lugs on the top of the larger multipliers (3/0 upwards) are included for a harness to clip to. These are only used for the largest skate, sharks and big game species, and many are incorporated into fighting chairs for billfish. Playing big fish without a fighting chair, using a harness in stand-up style, is a popular modern tactic.

The Fox Stratos 12000S fixed spool reel.

FIXED-SPOOL REELS

Modern fixed-spool reels are far more compact and less gawky than those of the past, and the label 'tractor' or 'coffee grinder' no longer applies to the best of them, although there are many cheap models which, although they look the part, fail to deliver.

Fixed-spool reels are not commonly used from the boat in the UK, although they are favoured by lots of anglers on the Continent for uptiding. This is mainly due to the older design reels lacking any lifting or winding power – the multiplier is always superior in this respect. However, modern fixed-spools with better gears do bring a few advantages to boat angling, notably the faster retrieve, and because the

Fishing light is not always possible at sea, but carp angler Ian Chilcott proved a Fox carp outfit was tough enough to land a 30lb conger.

line comes off the spool without it revolving tackle sinks to the sea bed quicker, ideal in uptide casting situations in extreme tides. An increase in the use of fixed-spool reels for uptiding, in particular, is likely to occur as anglers discover their merits for boat match fishing.

Essential features to look for in a fixed-spool reel for boat use include the correct spool capacity. Many manufacturers adopt a similar sizing system to multipliers, with 5000 through to 9000 the ones most often chosen. Fixed-spools are not produced for heavy wrecking or big game fishing.

With casting distance less important, the line lay oscillation system is not so crucial as with shore models, although the more expensive reels with a superior line lay tend to feature ball-bearings and tough gears more suited to heavy cranking.

A front drag is generally favoured because it enables the spool to be locked down tightly for casting. The alternative is the rear drag, where the spool drag system is operated by a screw to the rear of the reel. In all cases when choosing a larger model for boat angling, especially uptiding, look for the type with a click setting front drag because these are easily adjusted and do not lock up.

One advantage of the fixed-spool reel is that spools can be changed in an instant, making a single reel more versatile because you can change the line size quickly without taking the reel apart and simply swap spools.

Left: The latest Fox Stratos 12000S was used by carp anger, Ian Chillcott to land this conger eel.

CENTREPIN REELS

Centrepins are the original drum reel design with a single one to one ratio retrieve, although modern versions have been refined with a drag system and gears – unlike the knuckle-busters of the past which included those made from wood like the original Nottingham and Scarborough models. The one big advantage of the centrepin is the retrieve rate. The larger the drum, the longer the length of line retrieved, and in years past large drum centrepins were favoured by match anglers and those fishing very deep water. Nowadays centrepin reels are not so commonly used and mostly are only used for sentimental reasons.

A brace of cod aboard Fox-sponsored charter boat, Brighton Diver.

Awide variety of makes of monofilament, fluorocarbon and braid lines are available and they offer a range of quality as well as diameter and breaking strengths. Lots of anglers find a line they like and stick with it. However, modern lines, especially the monofilaments, have a mix of different material content percentages which have allowed manufacturers to produce many options, including those for specific tasks. These range from soft, supple reel lines that lack memory and flow through the rings smoothly but have great knock strength to protect them, to the stiffer, tougher, more rigid lines used for hook snoods, leaders and rig bodies.

BRAID LINES

Braid lines in their modern form have taken the boat scene by storm, and if you don't use them in the boat you are missing out on some amazing fishing. Their lack of stretch and low diameter means less lead is required to hold the bottom, bites are more positive and lighter, softer rods can be used to improve angling feel and enjoyment. This revolution has sparked a whole new rod concept, with massive advances in sea angling finesse.

Braid line has brought enormous advantages to the boat angler but is not the answer to all angling situations.

In the past non-stretch lines such as Dacron and Terylene enjoyed some popularity, but never really caught on as the modern micro braids have. This is mostly due to the advances in the fibres that make braid, with several of the mixtures of Kevlar and other materials offering a thinner, stiffer, tougher braid which is less prone to tangling than the softer, limp Dacron and the first Dyneemas.

Before too long braid lines will be produced that have a specific amount of stretch, so that anglers can choose precisely what they want to suit the conditions. You simple buy a line with X amount of stretch per metre

Braid also brings big advantages in its lower diameter for strength, which does away with the need for mono line rubbing or shockleaders, although some anglers still prefer the mono leader as an extra cushion to counteract braid's lack of stretch. This may be a good move if you are using a stiffer rod not designed for use with braided line, or are new to braid.

"Monos have lots of stretch and are still favoured for main line and hook snoods by many boat anglers."

Braid appears to break abruptly when pulling from a snag and this gives the impression that it is weaker than mono, which stretches and breaks more slowly. That's not the case. Braid's huge advantage is that it is extremely hard-wearing, and a spool will go from season to season without the need to replace it. Although initially it is far more expensive than mono, braid in the long term is by far the more economical line of the two.

BRAID'S ADVANTAGES

▪ Braid, with its low diameter and lack of stretch, does not oppose the tide as much as the equivalent breaking strain mono, allowing the use of lighter leads to hold bottom. Casting distance is obviously increased with a lower diameter line, which cuts the wind better. The less rapid decrease of spool diameter also improves the line's flow

▪ Lack of stretch means that every movement of the end tackle and hook is transferred to the rod tip, and striking actually moves the hook, whereas with mono the line stretch soaks up any such movement

▪ Braid lines do not coil like monofilament – they are more supple and less springy

▪ Braid lines is extremely tough and hard-wearing, with a lifetime as much as 20 times that of mono

BRAID FACT BOX

■ The early braid fishing lines were flat because they were produced for the construction of things other than fishing line. This caused them to float, making them mostly only suitable for spinning, but now round profiled braids specifically for angling, including sinking braids, are widely available.

■ Some of the latest braid lines (Fireline) include a thin outer coating, or are slightly heated to fuse the fibres together to give the line a softer feel and better flow. Clear and translucent braids continue to be developed. Other variations include braid lines with coloured bands throughout to act as markers, making fishing at a precise depth or distance simple.

■ Braid lines are made by twisting together polyethylene fibres to produce a strong, low diameter line with very little stretch. A 0.06mm diameter monofilament line has a breaking strain of approximately 1lb, but braid of the same diameter breaks at upwards of 8lb. This obviously offers many advantages.

■ European and Japanese braids are mainly constructed of Dyneema, while most of the American braids are made from the latest Spectra fibres, which are more expensive. They are similar, although Spectra claims to be 10 times stronger than steel, as opposed to Dyneema's five times. Both fibres are used in other applications, notably surgical stitching, industrial rope and bullet-proof vests.

BRAID'S DISADVANTAGES

■ Braid does not cast well on a multiplier because coils bed into one another when the line is stressed, causing the line to jam in the coils on the next cast. It performs best with a fixed-spool for casting, and Continental uptiders favour the fixed-spool for this reason, plus the fact that a lead will sink far quicker and be less restricted off a fixed-spool reel than a multiplier

■ Bites using braid are magnified, and this can prompt the angler to strike too often and too soon

■ Using braid line when fishing among groups of anglers who are using mono is considered antisocial, because a fine diameter braid will slice through mono if the two meet in a crossed line situation

Below: Braid has a low diameter per breaking strain, a lack of stretch and high abrasion resistance making it perfect for boat angling.

29

MONOFILAMENT LINES

Monofilament means 'single strand', and mono line is made by melting polyamide (nylon in pellet form) which is stretched to form a long continuous strand. Further stretching results in a range of diameters, and other treatments include the addition of colour or abrasion-resistant coatings.

The polyamides have undergone changes in recent times and modern mono line is superior to that of several decades ago. It still stretches, but is generally tougher and lacks the coil memory of the originals.

Monofilament will always be the choice of many sea anglers because the stretch is like a safety valve. Because it has been around for a long time it is also available in a larger range of diameters, breaking strains, colours and spool loadings. Other advantages include invisibility and cheapness –purchased on bulk spools it can be replaced regularly to ensure it is always in the best condition.

The diameter of a mono line determines its breaking strain, and it is this factor that is most important

to the angler. Thin lines oppose the tide far less than thick lines. At the same time, line strength is important in terms of the fish sought or the sea bed conditions, and so some thought must be given to the most practical line breaking strain to use in each situation. Most boat anglers carry several reels loaded with different

"Fluorocarbon has been largely ignored by sea anglers but it has superb knock strength, ideal for low diameter hook snoods"

diameter lines for different fishing methods, venues or species.

LINE COLOURS

Monofilament and braid lines are available in a wide range of colours, including bright day glow. Clear or white opaque mono lines are generally

preferred for clear water, while the brighter coloured lines are sometimes used for snoods or leaders and are considered useful in crowded charter boat angling situations when lines can become crossed and tangled. It is very much a personal choice, although the majority of anglers prefer clear line, judging by the sales figures.

Colouring mono line does weaken it slightly, although this is not regarded as significant. Among the colours, red is the first of the spectrum to lose its visibility under water and some anglers favour it for mainline and snoods because of this. However, sea anglers will often be fishing in very deep water where light does not penetrate, or in a pea soup sea full of mud and silt where even the brightest colours cannot be determined.

My opinion is that sea fish are not educated in terms of line colour or hooks because, once caught, most of them are killed. In catch and release situations fish may learn a little although, as proved by commercial longlines in deep water, bright orange cuttyhunk proves just as effective as clear mono, if not more so.

Line colour matters little as long as you are confident about using your favourite brands.

WIRE LINES

Less popular nowadays since the introduction of braid lines, wire is still used around the world for fishing lures deep in a strong tide, a notably popular method for catching American striped bass. Here the wire line is coloured at intervals so that the depth the lure is fishing can be set easily, while wire's total lack of stretch improves bite indication and the hook set. A disadvantage of wire is that it kinks easily, so special care needs to be taken when using it.

Alan Yates caught this striped bass out of New York on wire line.

"Big fish will find out any weakness in your line or knots."

Tackle boxes for boat fishing are generally more compact than those for the shore, simply because of the limited space and the lack of need to carry them far from the car boot. Cantilever tray systems are popular, while some anglers used the smallest version of the basic shore-style seat box. Large cool boxes, tackle bags, or either combined with a bucket, are commonplace. Boat tackle in general is heavy – leads, pirks and lures especially – and these are can be stored inside an extra bucket, making them easy to carry around.

The cantilever or toolbox style of tackle box allows easy access to the many items of kit, but a rogue wave or splash can quickly fill it and its precious cargo with corrosive salt water. They are also prone to spill in a moving boat. For this reason many anglers prefer the more expensive purpose-made waterproof style of tackle box, rather than the cheap supermarket toolbox.

A seat box, of course, offers a seat which may come in handy when travelling between fishing marks. The bigger ones will also store your tackle, bait and lunch in a dry, secure place.

TACKLE BAGS

Some of the most elaborate tackle bags aimed at boat anglers include a solid rubber base, and are fully waterproof. A bag may be a better option than a box, simply because it can be stowed far more easily into a boat or car boot, where it takes up less space. The downside is that items are stowed on top of each other, and you need to search through the top layers to reach the bottom, although many bags have a host of side storage pockets and are much more manageable.

RIG WALLETS

A rig wallet is not just for rigs! The standard type will include a dozen or more sealed plastic compartments, and most boat anglers go for the longer wallets with room for boom rigs. Capacity can be increased by storing rigs in separate sealed plastic rig bags. Wallets may have Velcro or zip seals, the latter being prone to corrosion.

"Keep your tackle compact and tidy in a tackle box with a waterproof accessories box for the small items and a rig wallet for traces, lures etc."

*The Fox
Deluxe Rig Wallet*

In recent times shore anglers have adopted the rig winder system for storing rigs and this is equally at home on a boat, the biggest advantage being that rigs can be removed from a winder without tangling. Even boom rigs can be stored on the largest diameter winders.

BAIT AND LURE BUCKETS ETC

A bucket is useful for carrying your bait and your catch. It can also be a handy way to carry large pirks, lures and heavy leads so they don't tangle up and remain accessible. Simple hang the lures via their hooks around the inside rim of the bucket.

TACKLE TIPS

* Booms are difficult to store because of their length, although a few large rig wallets will accommodate long booms, and winders can also be used for the compact metal booms. Another system is to store the longer booms in clear plastic tubes.

* Hang heavy pirks around the inside of a medium sized bucket for access and safe carriage.

* Feathered rigs are a pain to keep tangle-free - wrap them around a rig winder or several lengths of inch-diameter plastic conduit taped together.

GAFFS AND NETS

Many of the modern charter boats have adopted the big game idea of a trapdoor in the stern or gunnel though which to land large fish – it is physically impossible to haul 200lb of common skate over the gunnel without using gaffs. Such doors also allow wheelchair access to the disabled.

Most charter boat skippers will supply and operate a gaff or net and it is increasingly common for large nets to be used because of the increase in catch and release fishing. Even the largest species like conger can be netted. Gaffs are convenient, and their use has been refined to cause fish minimum distress.

Aboard a charter boat, take directions from the skipper, who will be well versed in netting or gaffing large fish. Aboard your own boat, the trick is to take your time. One hit with the gaff is enough, whereas wild swipes are the way to lose the specimen of a lifetime. Always make sure the gaff is stowed safely and to hand in case it is needed, but keep the point protected when not in use.

FLYING GAFF

Flying gaffs may be considered barbaric by some, but they are used commercially for the very large game species overseas and for the difficult to manhandle giant species such as halibut, common skate, shark and tuna. A barbed head that breaks free is attached to a rope, which may then be used for towing large fish inshore without the need to bring them aboard the boat.

TAILER

Some boat anglers and charter skippers use a tailer to land large species like tope that are to be returned. This is basically a lasso on the end of the gaff pole which goes around the tail of the fish before it is hauled aboard. Commonly used for shark and tope, its conservation value has been questioned because of the pressure it puts on the fish's internal organs, but many still employ a tailer for its convenience.

FISH LANDING TIPS

If you have a large fish on, take your time and make sure your reel drag is loosened. The sight of daylight or a touch with the net can set some fish off on their way back down to the bottom, and lots of big fish are lost close to the net because too much pressure is put on the hookhold or line. On a busy charter boat, don't crowd around the angler with the fish or the skipper with the net – give them plenty of room and if necessary get your rod and tackle out of the way.

ROD ACCESSORIES:

HARNESS

Shoulder or back harnesses common in big game fishing and in most cases are part of the fighting chair itself. However, in recent years stand-up harnesses have gained in popularity for those that want to fight a large fish out of the fighting chair – standing up.

LINE DEPTH COUNTER

Although a line depth counter is included in some models of multiplier reel, usually the motorised type, others can be clipped on to the rod with the mainline running through them. They are used to measure the depth at which your tackle is fishing, especially useful when fishing with lures in midwater or over a deep water wreck, when you need to keep clear of the structure. Once the feeding depth of fish is known, repeat casts can be made to the same depth.

BUTT PADS

Padded butt pads protect the hip and groin when pumping very large fish, and are usually on a waist belt with the rod butt slotted into an opening. The groove in the rod butt fits into an internal steel bar called a gimbal, which keeps the rod in position and prevents it twisting, offering more security and help with the retrieval of the bigger fish.

A net is considered more suitable for conservation for most species but on occasions the gaff still has a place.

If you have to use a gaff, hook the fish away from its vital organs etc, under the chin for instance.

There are two main priorities when selecting clothing for fishing from a boat. The first is safety, and nowadays anglers choose a flotation suit for this reason. The second priority is comfort and mobility. Staying warm and dry is essential, especially during the winter.

Choice of a one-piece or a two-piece suit is usually decided by the type of fishing. Deep water wreckers will choose the best of the one-piece flotation suits, while the inshore dinghy angler may be more likely to go for the two-piece for mobility's sake. In either case the suit's flotation rating is given in Newtons and is subject to the British Standard and DTI regulations. However, a flotation suit is considered only as a buoyancy aid – a full life jacket or vest is more efficient in terms of staying afloat.

During the summer a full flotation suit may be deemed unnecessary because of the heat, and some anglers end up using theirs as a seat. Not a good idea!

Sink or swim! – a Life jacket is essential boat angling wear.

The alternative is a life jacket or vest, and nowadays there are a host of lightweight harness-style life jackets that inflate automatically on contact with water. One word of warning –

"Never wear anything over a self inflating jacket!!"

Go for quality waterproofing – cheap waterproofs are rarely that good and many lose their water-repelling properties after their first wash. Look for trade names like Goretex and pay as much as you can afford. Many regular sea anglers go for yachting clothing from firms like Snowbee.

A variety of buoyancy aids and life vests are available for the boat angler.

Plenty of pockets, including internal ones for your valuables with Velcro and zipped seals to keep the water out, are of huge benefit.

REMEMBER - a warm, dry angler is an alert angler.

A floatation suit keeps the angler dry and acts as a buoyancy aid.

Most good flotation suits are supplied with a body harness to ensure that the suit does not ride up in the water. This is an essential aid to safety. Other features include bright day glow colours and a whistle. For durability, a padded knee area is essential. Most suits have a detachable hood, stormproof cuffs and a high collar.

It is not compulsory to wear a life jacket when afloat around the UK, although it is in Ireland.

Chapter 2
Boat Angling Basics

SPECIES SEASON CHART *regions vary between inshore & offshore*

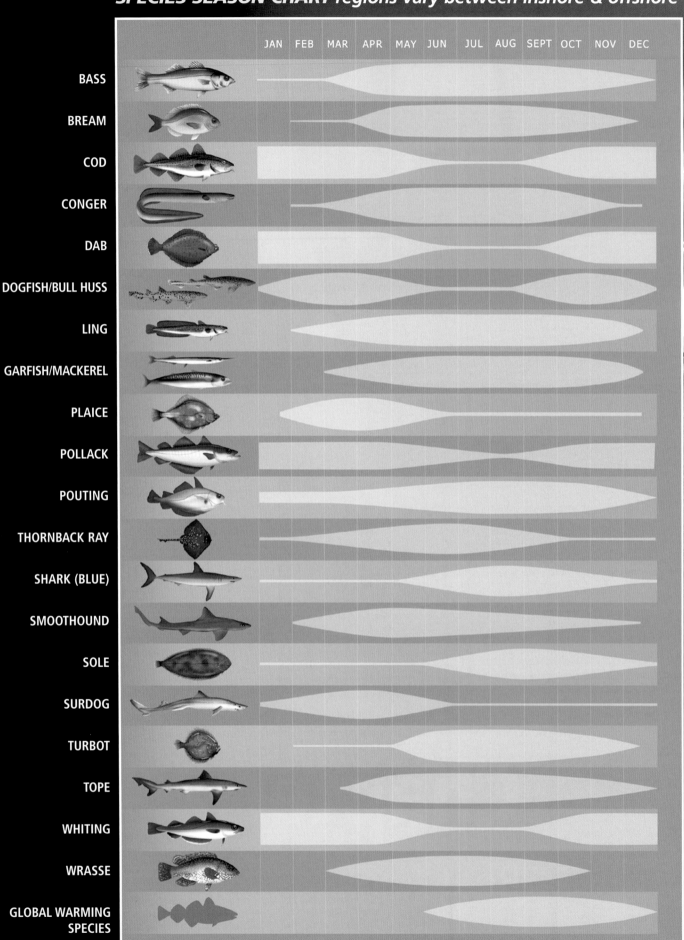

	JAN	FEB	MAR	APR	MAY	JUN	JUL	AUG	SEPT	OCT	NOV	DEC
BASS												
BREAM												
COD												
CONGER												
DAB												
DOGFISH/BULL HUSS												
LING												
GARFISH/MACKEREL												
PLAICE												
POLLACK												
POUTING												
THORNBACK RAY												
SHARK (BLUE)												
SMOOTHOUND												
SOLE												
SURDOG												
TURBOT												
TOPE												
WHITING												
WRASSE												
GLOBAL WARMING SPECIES												

The John Dory is one of the rarer species caught around the UK and an increasing number of even rarer species are showing during the global warming months between June and November.

The diverse range of species, venues and fishing methods required to catch fish from the boat around the UK produces a complex mix of tactics and tackle that can vary from region to region, and from season to season. No angler can never learn all there is to know about fishing around the UK – it is a continual learning curve – but one secret to success is to remember what you have experienced. Ninety per cent of anglers fall at this hurdle.

I have spent my life writing about sea angling, but each season anglers need reminding of the tactics, rigs and baits required to catch a particular species at a particular time of year. So many of them simply forget what they did last year!

There is no shame in writing down in a diary what, where, when and how you were successful. Another simple route to getting results is to copy other anglers, and that works on lots of occasions as long as you follow the successful ones! They probably copied someone else in the first place and to some extent very little is really new – ideas, tactics, methods and tackle are recycled, revamped and improved over the years.

In time, experience will tell you not to expect success on every trip, and that unless you follow the basic rules you will not be successful at all. In this and the next chapter I am going to deal with the nuts and bolts of boat fishing around the UK – all the things that can be learned to improve your catches. But there is one factor I cannot influence, and that is your instinct to fish, which cannot be learned like the alphabet.

The best anglers have a natural talent, their skills have been honed by experience and they react instinctively. Nothing beats a hunter's brain!

Fish location is a key to boat fishing success, especially when you consider the wide expanse of the ocean and the obvious odds of finding fish via merely random methods. There is a multitude of clues and ways to find the fish when aboard a charter boat, but this is normally done for you by the skipper.

Sea bed features are a natural attraction to many species of fish because they offer shelter and food. Sand banks, rock reefs, muddy gullies and other marine features are an obvious first venue choice, while man-made wrecks are home to many of the larger species. Perhaps Man's wars and disasters should be thanked for providing the fish with an impregnable shelter from the commercial nets – many wrecks are like an oasis in the desert for the fish and the rod and line angler.

The seasons have a major effect, and we describe some UK species as summer fish and others as winter fish. When these two different definitions overlap the result can be a fish bonanza. Generally this is during the autumn, as early as September and as late as December. Global warming and the change in seasonal temperatures has also had an effect in recent years, while the arrival of the winter, which is always a gradual north to south progression around our coasts, means some regions fish better for longer than others.

SEABED FEATURES SHOWING FISH LOCATIONS

POLLAC⁰ ETC.

CONGER

Listen to your skipper when drifting over a wreck – with his knowledge and electronics he will be able to tell you when to expect fish or when to reel up a few turns to avoid a snag.

Your choice of venue is often a make or break decision, so give it lots of thought and try to rely on facts rather than rumours or gossip. Remember, half the enjoyment of angling is talking about it afterwards, and many of us like to embellish and exaggerate.

Other major factors that affect the presence of a species or the ability to get afloat to get at fish is the weather, especially wind direction and strength. Some winds are never very productive,

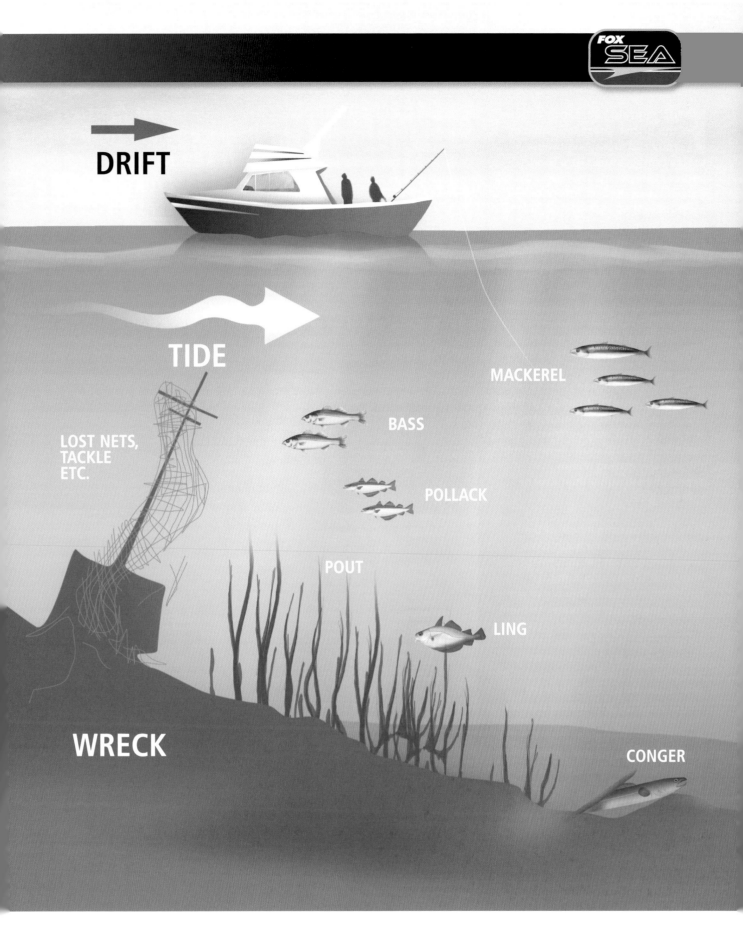

DRIFT

TIDE

MACKEREL

LOST NETS, TACKLE ETC.

BASS

POLLACK

POUT

LING

WRECK

CONGER

others nearly always are. Overall, an east wind for a prolonged period can kill sport completely, while a hint of north switches the fish on. Around much of the south and west coast any wind from west or south is productive, but often accompanies a rough sea.

Left to fend for themselves, most small-boat owners will eventually find fish, if only as a last resort by following the other boats. It can all become very technical, but fish habitat is basically controlled by seasons, food, spawning behaviour and instinct.

Find them and the challenge really begins. There is a world of difference between putting a boat over the fish and actually catching them. Of course, a bait among hungry fish will catch more than a bait on a barren seabed. Around a crowded wreck, fish compete for food and may be easier to catch.

ish migrate constantly around the British coast to spawn or move to more favourable water temperatures or a food source. This means that tactics and bait must adapt accordingly. One method will never be enough! The main seasons and species are predictable, although warmer summers and global warming have had an effect, and in many cases seasons of species overlap. Nowadays there is the ever-present chance of a surprise catch, either a rare species turning up out of the blue or species being late or early.

Here is a rough guide to what to expect through a typical year, bearing in mind that the daylight length, air and water temperatures do progress from south to north and north to south throughout the seasons, making this an approximation rather than a set of cast-iron rules.

MAY: The increasing length of the daylight and sunshine hours has a major influence on fish movement and migration, as do rising water temperatures. The further out to sea you go, the deeper the water, so there is less light penetration and it takes longer for the water temperature to change, which is why many extreme wrecking marks fish much the same all year round. However, inshore the arrival of spring prompts the summer species to return. The shore crabs peel their shells, and returning bait fish like sandeels, sprats, mackerel and whitebait attract smoothhounds, bass, codling, plaice, rays and many more.

JUNE & JULY: High summer sees the arrival and spread around the UK of the major species including mackerel, pollack, bream, ling, tope, smoothhounds, huss, rays, garfish, bass and plaice. The small bait fish and the mackerel are followed by the major predators as they move north. On the west coast of the British Isles the Gulf Stream speeds the species surge north, while on the east coast the cold North Sea slows the northern migration. A big plus of the calming summer weather is that those far-off wrecks can be reached, and for several months the calm seas give ready access to these

marks for charter boats and inshore dinghies.

AUGUST: This can be the bumper month for boat anglers, the settled, often balmy weather being great for getting afloat. Far-distant wrecks produce their crop of ton-plus conger eels, giant ling, pollack and cod. Regional temperatures and the sunshine can have an effect on the range of some species, but generally most species are reaching the limit of their northern range. In the north this can be one of the best months for mackerel and the species that chase them.

"Being in the right place at the right time is key to catching fish on a majority of occasions."

SEPTMBER & OCTOBER: Usually a time of plenty in most regions, with the summer species starting to overlap the returning winter cod and whiting. The mix of migrating fish on the way to their spawning grounds can bring spectacular results, and this period is the best in most regions for specimen

Late summer and autumn is a time when most of the fish species are present around the UK and the weather is usually good so make the most of it!

fish. It's also the time that most of the unusual or rare species appear.

NOVEMBER & DECEMBER: The bigger bass and cod feed heavily on their way to their winter spawning grounds, especially in the south and west, often moving inshore in range of the dinghy anglers. The weather changes in many regions at this time, and sea anglers have to contend with low temperatures and the weather. Look for the midweek calm days, windows in the weather when the most flexible anglers can get afloat and reap rich rewards!

JANUARY: Peak season for cod in many regions, although as the temperature falls and weather deteriorates catches fall off, but some really big fish are possible from the deepest wrecks if these are reachable. This is a time when most of the mature fish move away or offshore to spawn. A day afloat between the gales can still reap rewards, especially for fast wrecking charter boats.

FEBRUARY: In many regions the weather has the biggest effect on catches and boat fishing may stop altogether, skipper and owners taking

the opportunity to refurbish boats and equipment. Others switch to the sheltered estuaries in search of rays, while everywhere catches move away from cod towards the rays, dogfish and whiting. This is the month to book your charter trips for the summer – leave it later and you will be disappointed!

MARCH & APRIL: Spring codling and increasing ray stocks, plus the hungry, recently spawned plaice are major targets as the sunshine improves sport daily. This is the time to prepare boats and tackle for the coming season.

Access to the sea is not possible from many harbours and slipways during the spring low water. Look for a venue with access at all tides.

The huge amount of water movement caused by the tides has a major influence on boat angling success. The world's seas are influenced by the gravitational pull of the sun and moon, and this produces a surge of water around the globe as the planets rotate. Water depth and speed is altered constantly by this tidal surge. Two high tides (flood) and two low tides (ebb) occur in every 24 hours, and these advance in time as the Earth spins and the position of the sun and moon change.

Because this is a consistent movement, tides times and heights can be predicted accurately and tables can be prepared years in advance. Water depth and the shape of the land mass also have an influence on the tides' speed and power as water is funnelled and directed around headlands and through narrow straits.

The marine habitat and the behaviour of fish are controlled by tidal movement. Species use the power of the tide to travel to feed or lie in ambush, and in general the stronger the tidal movement, the more marine activity there is, peak times during the strongest ebb or flood tides generally producing the best results. In some cases, though, especially in deep water, the weaker tides are the only times it is possible to anchor and fish a bait accurately into a wreck, or drift over the mark slowly enough to catch the fish.

The shorter, weaker tides are called the neaps, and these occur when the gravitational pull is least strong, while the highest, most powerful spring tides occur when the combined gravitational pull is at its most powerful.

The high and low tide times in some ports can be critical in getting afloat in the first place, as many harbours are still dry at low tide. So a first step is to determine whether your chosen charter boat can get afloat at any time, day or night. Fortunately, in most of the major charter ports, marinas have been constructed to allow boat access to the sea 24 hours a day, while small-boat launching facilities, including slipways, have proliferated. Beware, because during the largest spring tides the water not only floods to its highest, but ebbs to its lowest, leaving slipways out of the water or a muddy sea bed to trail your car and dinghy over!

Tide Tips

You can buy a tide table showing the time of each low and high tide, plus its height, from most tackle shops. Armed with this you can select the best tides for fishing, usually the sets of spring tides. Consult your charter skipper for advice, and if fishing from your own boat the local dinghy/yacht/boat club could be a good starting point to finding suitable tides for launching and fishing. Part of the fun of fishing from your own boat is discovering these facts for yourselves, and although generations of anglers have copied each other, this is without doubt the safest and most successful action plan.

The beginner can start out buying ready- made terminal rigs from the tackle shop, and although these are often a stop gap measure they can be adequate for the novice. However, anything mass produced in a Far Eastern factory or the back of the tackle shop is never going to be totally suitable for the plethora of boat fishing scenarios around the UK and sooner or later the angler will want to construct his own rigs. But where does he start – copy a shop rig?

Think of it as giving someone a blank canvas and pencil. Few, if any, would produce a masterpiece and most attempts would be laughable. Building terminal rigs is like that, a disaster waiting to happen, so before we get into the actual construction of rigs let's start with an explanation of the various components that go into making them.

"The best terminal rigs are always the simplest designs"

To the newcomer, rig accessories can be confusing, especially because no two anglers have the same opinions on what is best. Hundreds of old and new ideas produce a mismatch of accessories behind the tackle shop counter. Where do you start, and which are for what?

Terminal rig accessories change with fashion, so it does pay to keep an eye open because some great improvements and advances are always taking place.

A standard strength system does, however, apply to boat angling accessories, and this dictates their size. Stronger modern materials have promoted lighter, more compact accessories, although there remains a standard strength rating that the angler needs to stay within. Accessories for UK boat fishing need to be a minimum of 20/30lb breaking strain, stronger for the bigger species or uptide casting, up to a maximum of 80/100lb for sharks and big game fish.

THE SIMPLEST RUNNING LEDGER BASIC RIG

Standard boat fishing terminal rigs are fairly simple, which is why they are so effective, although there are anglers who would wish to complicate matters, and match anglers do so because of their need to fish with a maximum of three hooks. But for the freelance boat angler who most of the time wants to fish with a single or a maximum of two hooks, rigs are uncomplicated and uncluttered with accessories. Basics are a connection link for the lead, a swivel for the hook length to prevent it being twisted and damage by a spinning fish, and a link and swivel combination or similar to attach the rig to the main line. Other than that, there can be add-on ideas to improve presentation, prevent wear and tear or tangles and help you catch more fish.

MAIN LINE

SWIVEL BEAD

ZIP SLIDER OR PLASTIC BOOM

30lb PLUS

LEAD

BUFFER BEAD

SWIVEL

CAN ALSO BE CONSTRUCTED WITH SWIVEL LEAD LINK

LEAD

CLIPS AND LEAD LINKS (right)

Used to join rigs to the main line or leads to rigs, a wide range of clips and links is available, some resembling a Chinese puzzle. Size and strength are the most important consideration – giant clips are not advisable because they increase the possibility of the hook snoods tangling around them, and they catch weed. There are many types of link including the popular Genie design, as well spirals and speed links. Oval links are also popular because they are small, but they are not always thumbnail friendly or quick to use when fingers are cold. The American snap link is a long-time favourite, but beware – the wire version is prone to opening out under pressure, making it suitable for leads only, so select your connection links for lures and rigs with extra care.

FOX SEA

COASTLOCK SNAP SWIVELS # 3/0

49

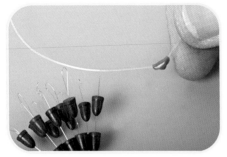

Baits need to be presented free from a tangle of rig line.

RIG OR BAIT STOPS

These are sliding rubber stops that can be passed on to the rod or snood via a wire loop. They can act as bait stops in conjunction with a bead or sequin to prevent worm baits riding up the hook snood away from the hook as the rig sinks. They can also be used to trap swivels and beads in position on a rig, or as a small buffer for the lead link on a flowing trace.

Fox Rig Stops have a multitude of functions and can be pulled on to the rig body line using their wire loop attachment. Once fitted Fox stops can be moved along the trace body line to suit requirements.

ZIP SLIDER OR SLIK SLIDER BOOMS

These are small mini clip/boom accessories made of plastic. They have lots of uses and are among the most popular rig accessories for boat anglers. Easy to assemble and use, they are great for fishing a single hook trace. Many charter skippers leave rods ready rigged with these small clip/booms sliding on the main line and stopped by a swivel. A hook snood is added prior to fishing.

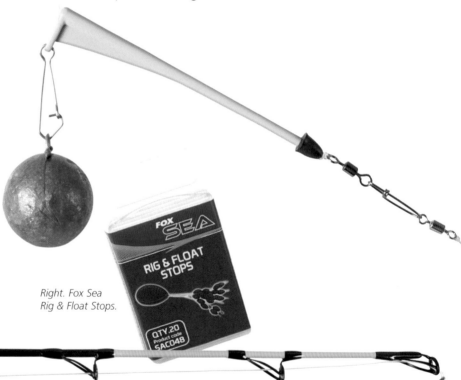

Right. Fox Sea Rig & Float Stops.

FLYING COLLAR BOOMS (above)

These are similar to the old-style French wire booms and are particularly useful for fishing any kind of lure or live bait on a long flowing trace. The original French boom has the advantage of being adjustable on the rig – it can be moved up or down. The flying collar is available from 10ins to 2ft long and has an eye at the top and bottom for the main line and lead. A good idea is to buy the type with a small swivel at the end of the boom, or to fit one yourself to prevent line twist when using long traces.

SAFETY OR TUBE BOOMS (above)

The recently introduced safety boom is an anti-tangle tubular boom which allows anglers to use longer traces. It is especially effective for bottom fishing or lure fishing with jellyworms and shads. It slides on the line to a swivel stop, and many types have a quick release for the lead, should it become snagged, Lengths available vary, with a 12ins-24ins boom sufficient for most methods of boat angling.

BUFFER BEADS (below)

Buffer beads are rubber beads that slot over the swivel to prevent the lead sliding down to a trace swivel and jamming up on the knot when used on a flowing trace. They are also ideal to put over the top swivel of the rig – particularly effective for mackerel feathering and match fishing, when a hurried retrieve can otherwise rap the swivel against the tip ring.

Left. Fox Sea Knot Buffer Beads.

ROTARY OR PLASTIC BOOMS (above)

The simplest of the plastic booms are of the rotary type, with metal versions also available. They are popularly used for inshore dinghy fishing with multi-hook rigs, paternoster style, so that baits are fished near the sea bed. The booms are secured between two beads and two crimps, or via rig stops or stop knots made from mono or Power Gum.

KNOT PROTECTOR SLEEVES (not shown)

These slide over knots, clips and swivels, protecting them and preventing cut ends of mono tangling rigs. Available in several colours, they add a professional finish to a rig.

POWER GUM (not shown)

This is a soft rubber line used for stop knots for securing rig accessories, or as float stops. Being rubber, Power Gum can be moved on the rig to re-position snoods and the like.

SWIVELS (right)

A large range of swivels is available, with many of the modern versions quite small for their breaking strains. They vary between the crane and diamond design to those with a round eye one side and a diamond the other, ideal for rig making. Available in stainless steel or matt, some, like the *FOX* variety, have an etched body to lower reflection and break up the profile of the swivel. In general, modern swivels are far more reliable than those of the past, and they actually swivel! Strength is the main factor when selecting swivels, with 30/50lb models for general rig making and up to 100lb breaking strain for heavier work. Three-way or Tri swivels are popular for simple terminal rig making because they can be placed in the rig's body line for an easy inline hook snood.

LUMINOUS BEADS (not shown)

Luminous and reflective beads can be charged up with a camera flash gun, a favourite ploy on the Continent. In many boat fishing situations in clear water, adding visual attraction to your hook snood will improve your catch, and not only for flatfish such as plaice. Fish from codling to pollack will react to movement and colour. Luminous beads can also be used to add weight to a hook snood to stop the bait fluttering about too much in the tide. They are available from tackle shops in a range of sizes.

ATTRACTOR BEADS (above)

These give you the option of different colours, and can be used like the luminous beads as attractors and to anchor snoods in a strong tide or simply as bait stops. You can also use certain colours on your rig to identify at a glance what type it is. Beads with an internal rattle are available, too.

BOAT AT ANCHOR

TIDE

TOO HEAVY LEAD WILL NOT MOVE DOWNTIDE

SEQUINS (right)

These come in a range of sizes and colours, and the circular type fits best on a hook snood. In my opinion red is best, and if you put six or more on a snood, by bending each one in an opposing direction you get more reflection. Terminal rigs that look as if they belong in the ballroom can be deadly, so don't be shy! Sequins also rustle and rattle, adding sound. They are available from dressmakers, haberdashery shops and most tackle outlets.

FLOATING BEADS (above)

These add buoyancy to baits and can be used to lift them out of the reach of crabs – a ploy used by flounder anglers fishing the southern estuaries and harbours like Poole, in Dorset, where the winter population of crabs removes worm baits rapidly.

I particularly favour floating beads because they can be used to give the bait negative buoyancy. Fish swimming past move the bait, within the line of sight of flatfish, which have upward-looking eyes!

PENNELL HOOK CLIP (above)

This neat clip, designed for boat or shore fishing with a twin hook Pennell rig, slides on the hook snood, allowing the addition of the second sliding (Pennell) hook in seconds. It offers great versatility when the angler is using a two hook Pennell rig for large baits. You can change the hook size or replace a blunt hook in seconds without having to break down or replace the complete hook snood. upward-looking eyes!

SPINNING VANES AND SPOONS (below)

Silver and brightly coloured spinning vanes and spoons have long been known to attract fish, and the smallest silver vane added to a snood can help draw attention to a bait. You can trap a vane between two beads and secure it with silicone or a stop knot. The larger flatfish spoons are available in most tackle shops, with the Fox range of vanes available in dayglow and silver.

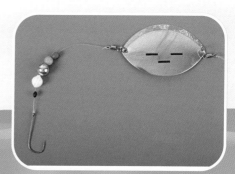

TOO LIGHT LEAD WILL END UP IN WRECK

GET IT RIGHT AND GET BAIT AMONGST THE FISH

FISHING AT ANCHOR
BOAT POSITION IS CRITICAL BUT TACKLE CAN BE POSITIONED NEAR WRECK WITH CORRECT LEAD AND USING TIDE TO 'TROUT' IT BACK TOWARDS WRECK

Sinkers are usually made of lead in a range of weights from 1oz upwards. In the recent past, with the exclusive use of monofilament lines, it was not uncommon for leads of up to 2lb to be used in the strongest tidal conditions. Tidal pressure on the line is what moves the lead and terminal rig, and obviously the deeper the water or (in the case of uptiding) the further the cast, the more pressure is placed on the line, weakening the lead's grip. Keeping your bait in position is one of the most essential tactics of UK boat angling, especially when the sea environment is hostile!

An increase in the use of braid lines has meant a general reduction in the weight of leads. Thinner braids catch less tide and have less stretch, enabling lighter leads to be used to hold bottom. However, the boat angler will still require a wide range of leads and these can be heavy, so it is wise to carry only those that you need for a particular trip. Most charter skippers carry a large selection of leads, and one I know colour-codes his according to weight, a great idea – his anglers can be told what colour to select at a given state of the tide.

PLAIN LEADS

Plain leads are all that the boat angler requires for downtide fishing, and 'plain' refers to a lead without grip wires. For uptide fishing, leads with grip wires are preferred to anchor the tackle.

For fishing in light tidal conditions in estuaries, or to allow the bait to roll or move with the current, a plain bomb-type lead down to 2oz is favourite. There are also a large number of other plain leads in different shapes that offer a range of different grips without the use of wires.

BOMB, PEAR AND TORPEDO

These are the most commonly used of the streamlined shapes, and allow a bait to be dropped to the sea bed in a direct line. A less aerodynamic lead shape may sink erratically and tangle the terminal rig or line. A bomb or similar shape can also be trundled downtide by the current with some help from the angler. A lead that is just heavy enough to touch the sea bed is lifted once it touches down so it catches the current, which pushes it back into the tide. This 'lift and drift' tactic is then repeated. With experience, it is possible to fish the bait some distance downtide of the boat.

CONE LEADS

The most common and practical lead for boat fishing in stronger tides is the cone lead which, because of its compact shape, sits firmly on the sea bed. This is the lead most favoured by charter skippers in weights between 8oz and 2lb for downtide bottom fishing with mono lines.

BALL, BULLET OR SPHERE

Spherical leads are not that commonly used, although more and more anglers are finding the bullet or ball lead ideal for wrecking because it is very streamlined in the water, offering little resistance, and some think its shape makes it less prone to snagging. It definitely sinks without tangling a long trace, and is unlikely to spook bass and pollack. There are several variations, ranging from a small drilled bullet (for float fishing or as an inline lead for fishing on the drift or freelining) to a bullet lead with a wire running

The ball lead has grown in popularity especially for lure fishing.

ACCESSORY TIPS

* Buying swivels and lead links in bulk is cheaper in the long run – small packets of 10 can prove expensive.
* Lots of the small accessories, including hooks, are sold in small plastic boxes which are ideal to protect the contents from corrosion.
* It is wise to carry only a small selection of accessories aboard a boat because salt spray can quickly penetrate even the best box and ruin the contents. Set accessories box and ruin the contents. Set up a rig-making box at home to keep your rig wallet stocked up
* Your accessories box should not spill items between compartments when tipped upside down – a simple point, but a jumble of accessories may mean you run out of an item without realising it.

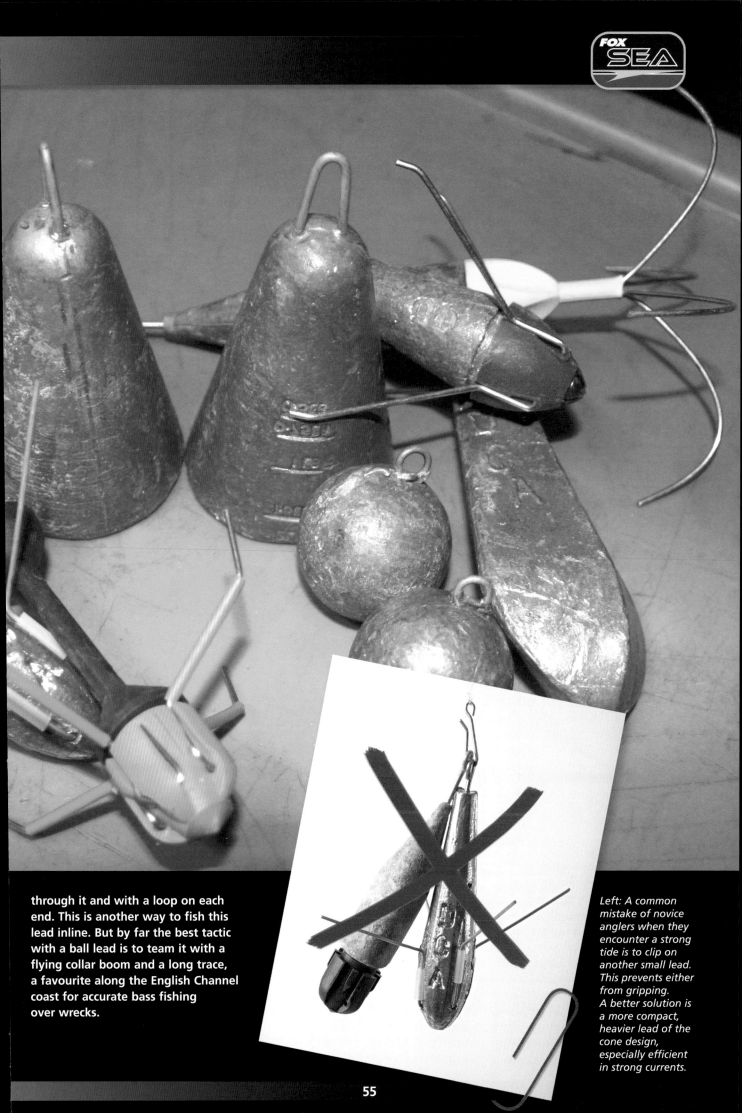

through it and with a loop on each end. This is another way to fish this lead inline. But by far the best tactic with a ball lead is to team it with a flying collar boom and a long trace, a favourite along the English Channel coast for accurate bass fishing over wrecks.

Left: A common mistake of novice anglers when they encounter a strong tide is to clip on another small lead. This prevents either from gripping. A better solution is a more compact, heavier lead of the cone design, especially efficient in strong currents.

Stone = 8oz
Yellow = 12oz
Red = 1 1/4lb
Green = 10oz
White = 1lb
Blue = 1 1/2lb
Gr... = 2lb

A fixed grip lead is essential for uptiding – This Gemini 6oz yellow head is one of the most efficient.

LEAD TIPS
* A FOX maggot box is a great place to store uptide grip leads in your tackle box, preventing wires from spiking probing fingers.

* The joint between the line and the eye of the lead is prone to damage, and for this reason it's advisable to ALWAYS use a lead link to join the rig line to the lead rather than make a direct connection. A lead link allows the joint to bend, and this keeps the knot clear of damage from rocks and rough ground on the retrieve. It also allows leads to be changed or removed easily.

WIRE GRIP LEADS

Wire grip leads are used mainly for uptiding, with the standard Breakaway (breakout) or fixed wire type favoured, depending upon the strength of the tide. These have four wire spikes to help grip the sea bed, and are produced commercially in various shapes and weights. Different wire thicknessess are available to suit the tide strength and type of ground being fished over. The Gemini lead type offers different coloured screw-in heads with various wire configurations (fixed and breakout) to match tide strengths. Wires are colour-coded blue (soft), red (springy) and stiff (yellow).

FEEDER LEADS (DEVICE)

Feeder leads include a compartment to keep delicate baits intact or to hold a selection of loose feed (ground bait), and are mainly used from the shore. However, the 'DVice', which has a section of clear plastic tubing behind the grip head to store the bait, is perfect for uptiding.

SINKER Q & As

Q: What weight of lead is best, and how many do I need?
A: In most cases aboard a charter boat the skipper will be able to supply the heaviest leads should they be required, although it's a good idea to check first. Always carry a limited range if fishing from an unknown boat. These leads can range from 2oz up to 1lb, enough to deal with most situations. Using braid main line does mean you can get away with far lighter leads in a strong tide.

Q: What should I look for when buying leads?
A: Avoid soft brass wire eyes or non-stainless wires that might corrode. When uptiding, the lead's wire length and springiness can affect grip. It's a good idea to check with the skipper or the local tackle shop what works and is the most popular uptide lead pattern required from the port you are fishing. You can adjust the tightness of a breakout wire by increasing the bend where it grips the lead. This alters the grip and release tension to suit the sea bed you are fishing. In extreme tides, when closing the wires tight is not enough to grip, wind an elastic band or small cable tie around the wires of a breakout lead. If that still does not hold, the alternative is a fixed wire grip lead. Check and re-bend wires of grip leads and breakout leads prior to every cast.

Some charter skippers and tackle dealers colour leads according to the weight. The feeder lead is mostly used for shore angling but can also be used for uptiding.

The rig and bait are placed in the tube, making the baited rig more streamlined, and the hook baits are forced out of the device when it his the water. The DVice is the perfect lead for uptiding on board crowded charter boats to avoid hook baits flying about when anglers are casting.

There are also combination leads, which offer a range of fitments including wires, long tails and various extended grip heads. These can be especially effective for the angler conscious of the weight he carries, because six leads have the combination potential of 12 or more different patterns and, like the Gemini range, come in a handy storage box.

Above: A feeder lead.

A Fox diamond file can be used to put an edge back on a dulled hook point.

The Fox range (Right page) includes all of the essential patterns and sizes used in the UK.

Hooks come in all shapes and sizes with hundreds of patterns available. List of hook type starting 6 o'clock clockwise:
•Eagle claw •Circle, red treble
•Limerick bend •Aberdeen
•Lure hook •Viking /Uptide
•Wide gape Aberdeen
•Hook with bait barbs •Blue Aberdeen
•Short shank •Circle

The most important modern breakthrough in the manufacture of hooks was their chemical coating. Instead of the age-old method of tumbling already sharpened hooks in a vat of enamel or similar coating, they are now coated chemically, which prevents them corroding quickly. Points are therefore not blunted as they were in the old tumbling process. This is not strictly speaking 'chemical sharpening', which is an advertising ploy. However, chemically plated or coated hooks are 50% sharper. I personally would not now use a non chemical-coated hook. A great test for a chemically etched hook point is that it will penetrate your thumbnail when your slide it over the nail – if it doesn't, BIN IT! Hooks for boat angling can range from a size 4 for tiny flatfish and bream to a size 12/0 for sharks. Then there is the little matter of the pattern. After a century-plus of sea angling there are thousands of hook patterns and types, although several companies (Drennan, Kamasan, Fox) have condensed the range down to the most practical, popular and efficient patterns. These are the most popular:

Fox Super Aberdeen Hooks

Aberdeen - Size 2 to 6/0
The Aberdeen is a long shank hook for general boat fishing, and perfect for all marine worms and frozen sandeel baits. The long shank not only makes threading worms easier, but helps with hook removal from your catch.

Fox Aberdeen Special Match Hooks

Match Aberdeen - Size 4 to 1/0
This lighter Aberdeen pattern in carbon steel is for competition fishing

using small or delicate baits. It is still very strong, so anglers targeting small fish like soles, garfish, bream, mullet, dabs, plaice and flounders are able to deal with the odd surprise specimen.

Fox Specialist Bass Hooks

Specialist Bass - Size 2/0 to 6/0
This lightweight forged carbon steel specialist bass hook with a razor sharp knife edged point, upturned eye, round bend and regular barb is perfect for fishing live baits for large bass. Hook baits may include live sandeels, joey mackerel and scad.

Fox Viking/Uptide Hooks

Viking/Uptide - Size 1/0 to 8/0
A tough, compact, short shank bronze pattern with a razor sharp knife edged point, neat eye and consistent barb. It is favoured for uptiding and general boat angling with chunky baits such as peeler crabs, squid and fish. The larger barb comes into its own when fishing for big fish like smoothhounds uptide.

Fox O'Shaughnessy Hooks

O'Shaughnessy - Size 6/0 to 10/0.
The ultimate big-fish , this is a large forged hook for the biggest species like sharks, tope, conger eels and rays, and perfect for carrying large bulky baits such as mackerel flapper, double Calamari squid and whole cuttlefish.

HOOK TIPS

■ The Viking pattern is ideal for use on a Pennell rig because of its compact medium shank length. Use a larger size for the sliding hook and nick this into the bait that is mounted on the lower hook for a 'hair rig' presentation style.

■ Most fish fatalities in sea angling are down to anglers using hooks that are too big. If you are fishing catch and release, bear this in mind.

■ Buying hooks in packs of five to 10 is expensive, and the dealers love the profit margin. Look for patterns sold in packs of 25, 50 or 100.

■ Bait barbs are totally unnecessary, a gimmick, and they cost you fish. Better bait presentation is obtained by threading the hook in and out of the bait accurately, using bait cotton and the eye of the hook to secure it.

■ The first thing the angler can do to improve his unhooking efficiency is to use long shanked hooks. Whilst short shanks are better for presenting some baits, long shanks are the easiest to remove, simply because there is more to grab hold of to twist, angle, bend or push.

■ Silver coloured hooks are considered the best for fish baits, but avoid stainless steel patterns – if lost in a fish they do not corrode.

■ Large hooks can be touched up and re-sharpened with a Fox diamond hook sharpener, but take care not to increase the angle of the hook point, which will blunt it.

HOOK FACT
After paying £200 for a rod and £100-plus for a reel, why do anglers use hooks more than once? Hooks can soon lose their points, especially the smaller patterns under a 3/0. Don't be a Scrooge, check and change your hooks regularly. The larger patterns can be sharpened, but often this changes the thin angle of the point or dulls its razor edge. If you are not careful you will end up blunting the hook point!

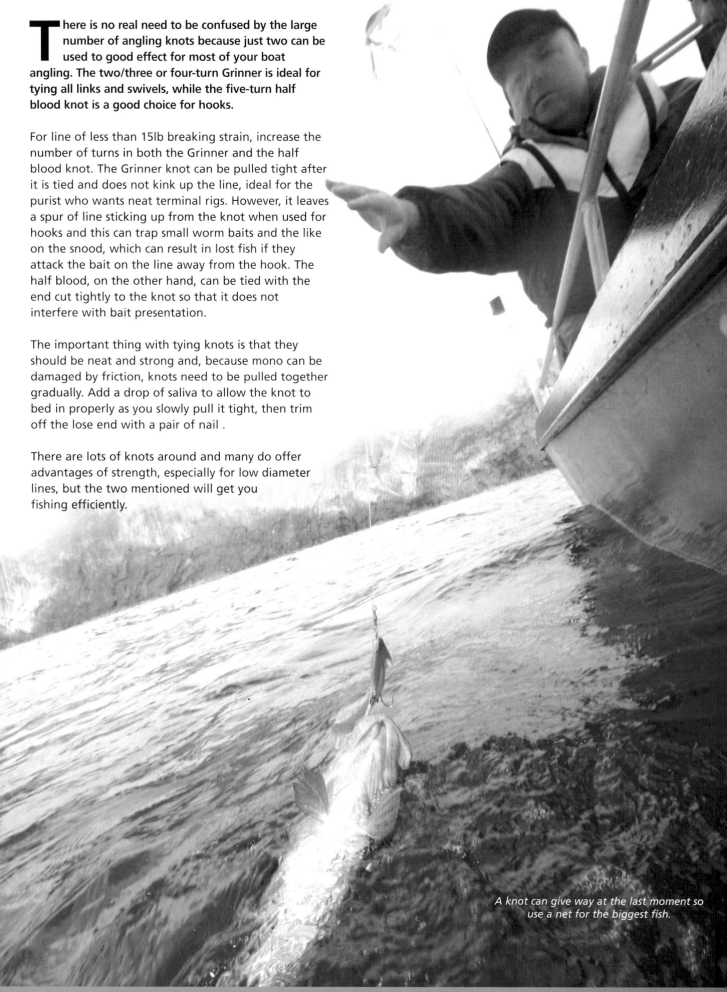

There is no real need to be confused by the large number of angling knots because just two can be used to good effect for most of your boat angling. The two/three or four-turn Grinner is ideal for tying all links and swivels, while the five-turn half blood knot is a good choice for hooks.

For line of less than 15lb breaking strain, increase the number of turns in both the Grinner and the half blood knot. The Grinner knot can be pulled tight after it is tied and does not kink up the line, ideal for the purist who wants neat terminal rigs. However, it leaves a spur of line sticking up from the knot when used for hooks and this can trap small worm baits and the like on the snood, which can result in lost fish if they attack the bait on the line away from the hook. The half blood, on the other hand, can be tied with the end cut tightly to the knot so that it does not interfere with bait presentation.

The important thing with tying knots is that they should be neat and strong and, because mono can be damaged by friction, knots need to be pulled together gradually. Add a drop of saliva to allow the knot to bed in properly as you slowly pull it tight, then trim off the lose end with a pair of nail .

There are lots of knots around and many do offer advantages of strength, especially for low diameter lines, but the two mentioned will get you fishing efficiently.

A knot can give way at the last moment so use a net for the biggest fish.

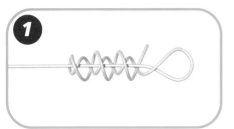

1

Left: First find a place to anchor the loop. You can use a rod rest, door handle etc. Its essential to keep the loop under tension. Now form the loop and twist twenty times, more loops for lighter mono.

Right: The shock leader is tied to the bimini loop via a two turn grinner knot.

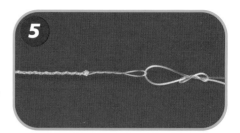

5

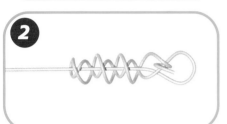

2

Left: Lock the loop off with a half hitch around one leg of the loop.

Right: Once the grinner knot is tied in the loop pull it tight slowly and the knot will form and lock into the loop.

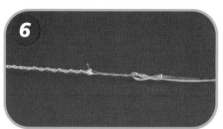

6

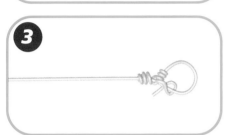

3

Left: Alternate half hitches on both legs of the loop, you can also tie a half hitch around both legs together.

Right: Trim lose ends of the knot with clippers and finish the knot by melting (blob) the mono ends with a lighter*.

*Please take care with this stage. This procedure should not be attempted by children under the age of 16 unless supervised by an adult.

7

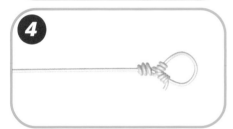

4

Left: The required number of half hitches to prevent the knot slipping is around six.

Right: The finished knot.

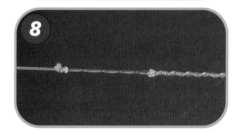

8

KNOT TIP

There is nothing worse than losing a leader while you are fishing, so here is a handy knot for making replacement leaders at sea. It is my own variation, and I use it mostly for uptiding with braid main line in emergency situations. It can also be used with tapered mono leaders, but not with parallel leaders of more than 40lb breaking strain. (Swapping reels is the answer to most lost leader situations, but if you want to stay with a reel that is catching, you have to replace the leader)

The lasso loop and whip knot can be tied quickly while you are fishing. Form a loop in the main line (in braid use a double overhand knot to tie the loop), then lasso the loop around the leader. Twist the leader back up the main line six times and then three to six times through the loop it forms. The turns need to be teased together very carefully, but they form a neat, strong knot which with practice is easy to tie.

CUT BLOOD LOOP
Simple way to construct a hook snood in a flowing trace

Forget the complicated knots, these 3 are sufficient for all situations

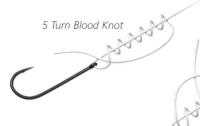

5 Turn Blood Knot

Tucked Blood Knot

3 Turn Grinner Knot

Are you looking for:

- **Expert advice articles to catch more fish**
- **Up to date news, regional fishing reports and gallery of latest catches**
- **Inside info on proven marks**
- **Comprehensive Charter boat and tackle shop directory**
- **Independent boat and tackle reviews**
- **Top competitions to win the latest gear**

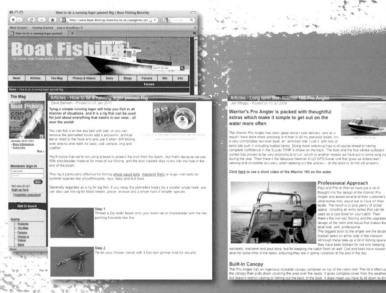

If yes, then
www.boat-fishing-monthly.co.uk
is for you!

Don't forget to sign up to the monthly e-newsletter, including exclusive website features and competitions, blogs, forums, galleries, news and what's in the latest issue of the UK's only dedicated monthly boat fishing magazine.

Chapter 3
Fishing Methods and Terminal Rigs

TIDE

COMPLICATED
RIGS AND
LARGE BAITS
CAN TANGLE
ON DESCENT

BOOMS AND
PRECISE RIG
DIMENSION
HELP AVOID
TANGLES

Nothing would appear simpler or more fun than anchoring a boat and fishing downtide from the stern, and indeed this is a major tactic of anglers around the UK. Problems can arise in positioning the boat accurately over the mark (a sandbar, gully or wreck), although modern electronics enable most to master the technique, while for professional charter skippers it becomes second nature.

Once anchored, the boat will ride on the anchor rope downtide and any tackle dropped from the boat will also be forced downtide – how far depends upon the weight of the sinker (lead) being used and the strength of the tide.

Problems start when the tide is strong and tackle and lines are swept downtide. On a crowded charter boat, lines from anglers in the bow can tangle with those fishing over the stern. Even when fishing downtide in a dinghy, the deeper the water, the greater the pressure is on the line. This is transferred to the rig and lead, and a heavier lead is the only

solution to keeping the tackle stationary. So the first consideration of downtide fishing is the weight of lead to use – 8oz will normally be sufficient although leads of up to 2lb are used on occasions.

Several factors will affect the control of the tackle, a major one being the diameter or type of main line. Braid or thinner monofilament will catch less tide and allow lighter leads to be used. Braid has become universally popular for downtiding because they are thin and lack stretch, remaining in direct contact with the rig. The 2lb leads of the past are no longer required when using braid.

One problem for the novice is that tidal pressure on the line will continue to run line off the reel spool and often he will pay out lots of line behind the boat, thinking his tackle is being towed downtide. In reality his tackle will be on the sea bed below him and a large loop of line will belly downtide behind it. This will nullify bite indication, and in some cases anglers' rigs are pulled in by others without them realising.

The correct technique for fishing efficiently downtide is to use just the right amount of lead needed to reach the sea bed, not too much so that it is anchored where it falls and not too little so that it is lifted off the bottom and swept downtide. The tackle just needs to be bounced downtide until it reaches a point where it anchors under its own weight. This will get baits away from the 'scare area' around the boat and away from other lines. It also means that the bait on the rig will be the first scent any fish swimming uptide will encounter! This is why the stern positions in any boat are always the premier spots.

Fishing downtide will always mean that the line is swept in a bow, cushioning bite indication, especially when using mono lines. The greater the line diameter, the longer this bow will be. Braid is especially effective for those fishing near the bow of the vessel because the tackle sinks directly to the sea bed and not so far downtide to tangle with the rods fished from the stern.

Cod remain a favourite species of the boat angler and they are one of the biggest specices.

Above: A 20lb cod is considered a specimen.

"When fishing on your own there is little risk of a tangle, but on a busy charter boat, especially with novices aboard, fishing down tide is asking for tangles."

DOWNTIDING

TANGLE

When fishing rigs downtide, all tackle/lines are forced into a narrow band behind the boat by the tide. This results in tangles as anglers retrieve. Mono line is forced further downtide than braid so position mono anglers in stern and braid nearer bow.

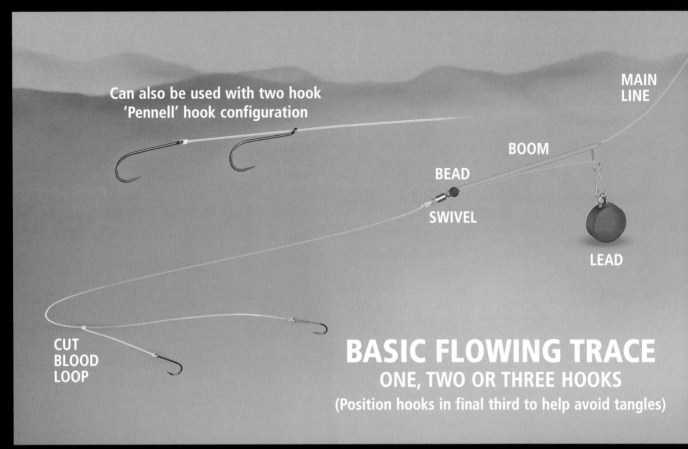

Can also be used with two hook 'Pennell' hook configuration

MAIN LINE

BOOM

BEAD

SWIVEL

LEAD

CUT BLOOD LOOP

BASIC FLOWING TRACE
ONE, TWO OR THREE HOOKS
(Position hooks in final third to help avoid tangles)

DOWNTIDING RIGS

The most important aspects of terminal rigs for boat fishing are their dimensions, snood lengths and lengths of the rig body between snoods being crucial to the rigs' behaviour on the sea bed. Overlapping snoods will tangle, and although casting is often not involved in boat fishing, the pressure of the water on a rig and the hook bait as they sink is often destructive in terms of tangles. So the make-up and dimensions of terminal rigs for boat fishing are critical, and this greatly restricts the range of rig configurations compared to those for shore fishing.

Because hook snoods and baits can and will spin around each other, getting the relative dimensions correct will make an enormous difference to the rig's success rate. A simple solution to tangles is to limit the rig to a single hook, or stick with proven designs. Complicated boat rigs look fine on paper and on dry land, but in practice rarely work efficiently.

One big advantage of not having to cast a rig from the boat is that the breaking strain of the line is not so

critical, allowing lighter rig body lines and hook snoods to be used. This permits better bait presentation and reduces tackle losses, because a lighter hook snood will break before the stronger main line. A practical compromise between the diameter and length of line being used minimises tangles, whereas stepping outside the standard parameters will result in even the simplest rig become tangled!

FLOWING TRACE

The simplest and most effective downtide terminal rigs is the straightforward single hook flowing trace. This is particularly efficient for targeting big fish with a single hook, or two hooks Pennell-rigged. It can also be used in multi-hook configurations with two or three hooks.

The beauty of this rig is that the hook bait trails or flows behind the lead and is hard on the sea bed, which is where most of the common species will be looking for food. Crucial in the construction if more than one hook is used is the spacing of the hook snoods. As a general rule, all hooks

should be positioned in the final half of the trace to prevent tangles as the rig sinks to the sea bed. An excellent compromise is to use just two hooks, widely spaced, greatly reducing the likelihood of a tangle.

The flowing trace can be connected to the main line in a number of ways, the most popular and efficient being the via the safety or tubular boom, or the very basic zip slider boom. The former keeps the trace line away from the lead and prevents tangles as the rig is dropped to the sea bed, especially effective for lure fishing over wrecks. The line is threaded through the tube of the boom, which has a rubber elbow to angle the boom out from the lead and a swivel attached to the end of the main line. A Fox rig stop attached to the line before the swivel acts as a buffer, and also allows the trace to be lengthened at will. The lead link on the safety boom includes a release mechanism which can be used for wrecking situations. Alternatively, a large swivel link can be placed over the plastic section of the boom between the rubber and the bend.

MONOFILAMENT PATERNOSTERS

The monofilament paternoster is the basis of many popular terminal rigs in sea angling, especially from the shore – it is easy to tie and not prone to tangling. However, it is not as effective from a boat for downtiding in all situations and is often only used for fishing strings of feathers and lures, or in conjunction with three booms placed close together.

For bottom fishing from the boat, the mono paternoster's main drawback is that if the body of the rig is made too long it presents baits up off the bottom, and many sea species will not readily take bait off the sea bed. Because of this a combination one up, one down mono paternoster

Three-way swivel

Fox Rig Stops

MONO PATERNOSTER

Can be constructed with beads and crimps or three-way swivels.

More refined 'adjustable' version using FOX Rig Stops.

is often the answer, with long snoods loaded with beads used to nail baits to the sea bed. Conversely, fishing for some species that do feed off the sea bed, such as garfish, mackerel, bream and school bass, longer hook snoods on a mono paternoster allow the bait to flutter back in the tide, into a wreck or reef.

The mono paternoster is generally constructed by trapping a small swivel between two beads and two crimps. Close the crimps lightly and the swivel hook snood positions can be altered. Alternatively, Power Gum stop knots securing all swivel positions allow the adjustment of hook snoods.

If you are constructing a three-hook mono paternoster the best choice is the two up, one down combination, but hook snood length and spacing is crucial to avoid tangles, especially when fishing in deep water.

BOOMS AND SPREADERS

Wire boom rigs have been around for years. In the past the angler realised the value of using such booms to prevent hook snood close together tangling with the main line and each other. The weight of the wire also helps present and keep hook baits hard on the sea bed. Booms are made to stand off the body of the

rig, allowing lighter hook snood lines to be used.

By far the most efficient multi-wire boom rig is the wire spreader, somewhat out of favour nowadays but still a force to be reckoned with in match fishing circles. The spreader comes ready-made in various configurations, including the two-boom helicopter style and the old standard two up, one down combination. Constructed totally in 28 SWG stainless wire, or in a combination of wire and mono,

"If you are in doubt about how to build a particular rig, buy one from the tackle shop and copy it."

the rig is a favourite among dinghy anglers for cod, whiting, dabs and plaice. The spreader presents three baits close together on the sea bed and can be bounced back in the tide without tangling. The glitter and noise of the rig is said to add to its attraction. For storage, a spreader collapses and can be stowed in a plastic tube or rig wallet.

Various other types of wire boom are available for single hook snoods. The oldest is the French wire boom, fished singly or in two or three-paternoster style. This is ideal for presenting three baits close to the sea bed without tangles, and their advantage over the wire spreader is that each boom's position can be altered and adjusted on the rig while fishing.

DOWNTIDING TIPS

* A plain lead will allow the rig to be trundled downtide in the current. Turn the reel handle or lift the rod at regular intervals to cause the rig, beads and baits to lift and flutter – this often gets a reaction.

* Some species will chase and devour a moving bait, others will only accept a bait nailed on the sea bed. For bottom fishing with the hook baits close to the lead, so they are on the sea bed, a flowing trace is the favoured rig. When fishing lures off the sea bed, a paternoster rig is preferred.

* The stern positions are always best in a boat fishing at anchor because the tackle can be fished further back from the boat, away from any scare area. Rods fishing in the bow positions that are allowed to trot back to the stern can entangle with the stern anglers, so in general it's wise to fish with a slightly heavier lead from the bows. Some sort of draw for boat positions, or a rotation of places, is always advised when fishing downtide in a charter boat because the stern positions offer so many advantages.

* Heavy leads sink quicker and are worth considering in deep water and strong tides to get to the sea bed quickly and stay there.

Big fish are sometimes hooked on rigs not intended for them, an excellent reason to make sure you use the best line and accessories.

The flying collar boom is an all-wire boom between 8ins and 2ft long. It is similar to the French boom but is fixed, rather than adjustable.

The most modern and effective boom for downtide fishing has already been mentioned, the tubular. The main line runs through the centre of the boom to a swivel to which the trace is attached. A buffer bead above the swivel prevents the boom jamming. Fished with a flowing trace with one, two or three hooks, it is especially favoured for lure and live bait fishing sink-and-draw style.

BOOM LEAD

A Continental system for fishing very shallow water, this is a lead sinker with two or three booms moulded into it. Hook snoods are kept short, with baits presented hard on the sea bed.

Metal spreader (also available in three booms)

French Boom

(Both are adjustable)

Modern Fox Wire Boom

BOOMS AND SPREADERS

Both allow the use of light line hook snoods without tanging

CASTING UPTIDE

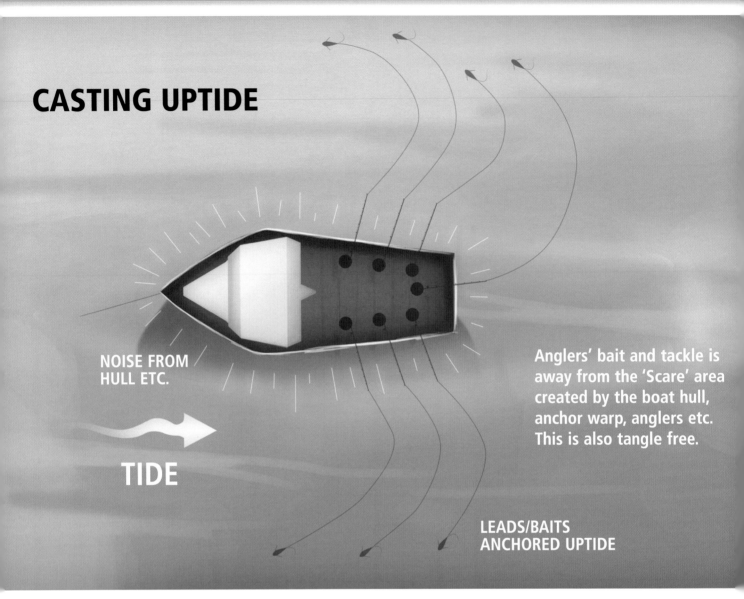

NOISE FROM HULL ETC.

TIDE

Anglers' bait and tackle is away from the 'Scare' area created by the boat hull, anchor warp, anglers etc. This is also tangle free.

LEADS/BAITS ANCHORED UPTIDE

Uptiding was first used by anglers fishing from charter boats in the Thames estuary, and is now one of the most popular and effective methods of fishing from an anchored boat in shallow waters around the UK and for bait fishing in other parts of the world.

An anchored boat sets up a 'scare area', and this and the capture of fish close to the boat can deter some species from coming close to the hull. Casting a bait away from the boat, either across the tide or uptide, gets the bait out from that scare area and also allows anglers in the boat to fish without tangles. This is a benfit often overlooked. The fact that anglers are casting away from the boat across and uptide gets line and terminal rigs clear of each other, as opposed to fishing downtide, when all the rigs are swept downtide into the same line behind

the boat. Experienced uptide anglers regularly use two rods each because of the efficiency of the tactic.

It's important to anchor the rig where it lands on the sea bed, and a range of wired grip leads are required to combat the strength of the tide. The breakout lead is suitable for light tide conditions, and the fully wired lead essential in stronger currents. Bites are signalled by the line dropping downtide as a fish pulls the lead free from the sea bed, and thanks to the belly in the line downtide striking is not required. The tactic is to reel in immediately the line slackens to pick up the weight of the fish and then pull into the fish, which in most cases will have hooked itself.

A short to medium-distance cast works most efficiently because a long length of the line in the water generated by a

long casts puts greater pressure on the hold of the lead. A simple overhead thump is generally all that is required, with 20 to 50 metres a sufficient distance.

Terminal rigs with bait clips are not always necessary either, although bait clips do make the rigs safer for boat casting because hooks are not left dangling on snoods to catch on things – despite the number one rule of boat casting being to only cast with the end tackle hanging outside the boat, accidents do happen.

FAVOURITE UPTIDING RIGS

With casting involved, uptiding terminal rigs are best kept simple, compact and streamlined, and lots of anglers prefer to use a single hook for safety and to prevent tangles. Uptiding is also viewed as a one- fish method, usually for the bigger species. There

are several favourite rig designs and in all cases it's the dimensions of the rig that are most critical. Over-long snoods will spin and tangle, swivels and clips will catch hook snoods. This being the case, popular rig designs are kept simple, to be efficient and tangle-free. As with downtiding, stick to the proven patterns and take extra care with the rig dimensions and their behaviour. If a rig tangles regularly you know you have it wrong, bearing in mind that an uptide rig can tangle during casting, as it sinks and as it is retrieved.

MONO PATERNOSTER

By far the favourite rig for uptiding is the one hook mono paternoster, of which there are several popular variations. A single mono paternoster made by trapping a swivel between beads and crimps is the simplest to construct and use. With a top clip for connection to the main line and a link for the lead, nothing could be simpler. However the rig has one disadvantage – the hook snood length is restricted so that it cannot tangle around the top clip. A popular and efficient variation of this rig is to tie the hook snood via a blood loop knot in the main line so that there is not a link above the snood for it to tangle with. The larger the blood loop, the longer the snood can be made. The next variation is called a 'running paternoster', and this involves the use of a 12ins-24ins length of line between lead and swivel. The main line goes through the swivel and is tied to another. The hook snood is tied to this second swivel, which means that a fish taking the hook bait will not feel the weight of the lead because the line will run freely through the swivel. When the paternoster rig involves two hook snoods, tangles are more likely. The most efficient rig design for two hooks is the one up, one down rig. One hook is on the rig line above the lead and the other one below.

LOOP RIG

The loop rig is a popular shore rig for long-range casting. However, it is just about the most compact of the rigs

CUT BLOOD LOOP RIG
Old, but still the simplest uptide rig

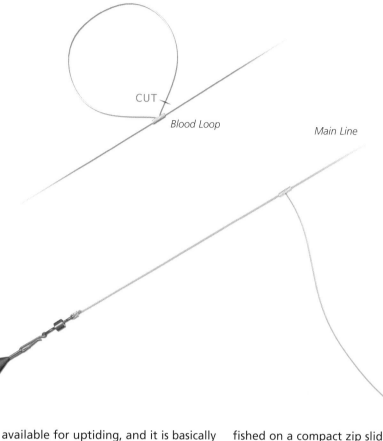

CUT

Blood Loop

Main Line

Hook

available for uptiding, and it is basically a clipped one up, one down rig.

FLOWING TRACE

Several types of flowing trace can be used for uptiding, and many anglers prefer a simple short flowing trace

fished on a compact zip slider or tube boom. A single hook on a 3ft-plus trace is the normal choice. For two hooks, extra length is required, although this does make the rig far more cumbersome to cast and more likely to tangle.

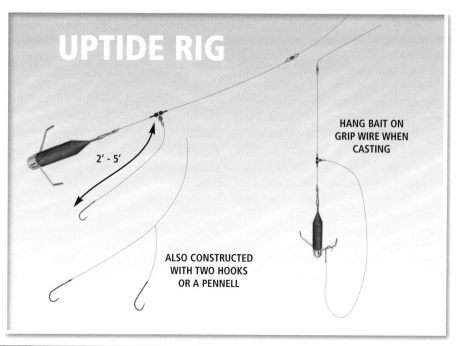

UPTIDE RIG

2' - 5'

HANG BAIT ON GRIP WIRE WHEN CASTING

ALSO CONSTRUCTED WITH TWO HOOKS OR A PENNELL

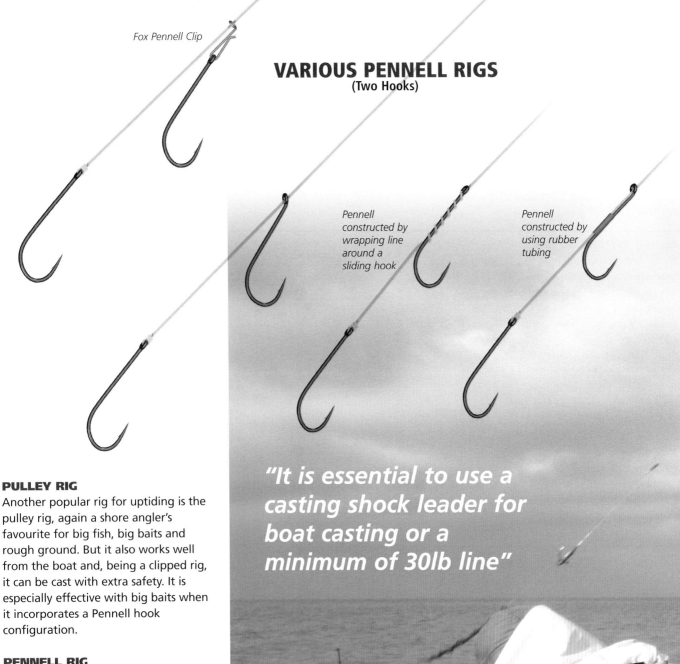

Fox Pennell Clip

VARIOUS PENNELL RIGS
(Two Hooks)

Pennell constructed by wrapping line around a sliding hook

Pennell constructed by using rubber tubing

"It is essential to use a casting shock leader for boat casting or a minimum of 30lb line"

PULLEY RIG

Another popular rig for uptiding is the pulley rig, again a shore angler's favourite for big fish, big baits and rough ground. But it also works well from the boat and, being a clipped rig, it can be cast with extra safety. It is especially effective with big baits when it incorporates a Pennell hook configuration.

PENNELL RIG

The Pennell rig is two hooks fitted to a single snood, and it can be used on any type of single bait rig. The idea is that when using a very large bait, a hook can be positioned at both ends, giving an increased chance of a fish being hooked. The Pennell configuration also helps to secure large baits in position on the two hooks and is often favoured for use with whole squid, cuttlefish or mackerel flapper baits, just for the secure presentation. A large bait on a single hook can often slide down the hook snood and hook shank to hang in the bend and block the point. This often happens when fishing deep venues in strong tides as the bait descends.

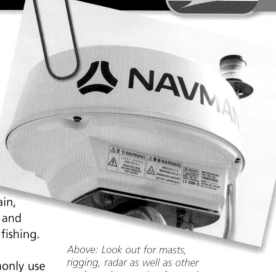
UPTIDE CASTING SHOCK LEADERS

A casting shock leader is sometimes required for uptide casting, but because casting is normally a simple overhead lob, heavy breaking strain shock leaders are seldom required. Most boat anglers manage with 30lb to 50lb leaders and many fish a 30-35lb breaking strain mono line straight through to avoid having to include a potential weak spot in the line, such as a leader knot. However, in the strongest tidal conditions low diameter lines combat the tide better, with a 15-20lb main line and 40lb leader often the best compromise.

Leaders are also used for the larger species to prevent species like sharks, that have a very rough skin, chafing or breaking through the main line if they roll on it or tangle in it. These are called 'rubbing leaders', and their diameter and durability are more important than their breaking strain. In the main, rubbing leaders are 100lb-plus and limited to shark and big game fishing.

Boat anglers using braid commonly use a mono shock leader to act as an extra cushion because of the braid lack of stretch, which makes it inefficient in some uptiding situations because of its lack of stretch. This puts more pressure on the lead, which may not hold. A compromise when using braid for uptiding is to use a short 15ft mono leader to act as a safety valve.

Above: Look out for masts, rigging, radar as well as other anglers when casting from a boat.

BOAT CASTING SAFETY AND RULES

Casting a baited terminal rig from a boat carries a number of dangers, and most charter skippers observe a strict procedure and enforce a few commonsense rules.

1. A shock leader should always be used to take the strain of the cast – a snap-off can be as dangerous on a boat as it is on the shore. Using a minimum 30lb main line is fairly common, and this will handle the average overhead lob cast. Power casting is not required in the boat and a very long cast will put more line in the water and catch more tide, so it's not necessary. However, for those in doubt about their casting skills, don't go below 50lb.

2. Never cast with the rig inside the boat. Hang it outside the gunnel, and always ensure other anglers are aware that you are casting. In the haste of fishing this is where accidents happen, so communication with others fishing is essential – a shout of 'casting' will alert all to your actions.

3. Beware of masts, rigging, radar, etc and do not try to cast if you are restricted for room.

4. Keep rigs compact, so that hooks and baits don't whiplash around during casting.

UPTIDING TIPS

* When using a single hook flowing trace, which is one of the most effective uptide rigs, hang your hook bait on the grip wire of the lead to shorten the length of the trace and prevent a whiplash effect which may damage the bait - this is also far safer.

* A heavy lead sinks quickly and will therefore hold further across or uptide. Once the lead has hit bottom, the angled line will pick up maximum tidal pressure. Allow the tide to pull the line from the reel spool so that it forms a bow downtide - this will help the lead to grip into the sea bed.

* Strength of tide dictates what type and weight of lead needs to be used to hold bottom efficiently. In many cases a standard breakout lead is ideal. Add an elastic band to the wires to improve its grip, but in extreme tides switch to a fixed wire grip lead. Don't be afraid to use a heavier lead.

* Don't sacrifice bait size to increase distance. The bait scent is the most potent weapon the angler has to attract the fish to the hook! Bait clips can be used to add a few yards, but are more important in terms of presentation and safety than distance.

* A heavy lead used in deep water will land on the sea bed close to where it enters. Too light a lead may well be too far downtide when it hits bottom, so that its grip is impaired by the angled pressure of the line. In all cases, casting slightly uptide to compensate for downtide movement is effective, like a shooter aiming in front of a moving target!

There are two main methods of fishing over wrecks – at anchor, downtiding baits into or towards the wreck, and drifting over the wreck with lures. Locating the wrecks and putting the boat over them we will leave to the skipper for this section – it is dealt with later in this book.

FISHING AT ANCHOR OVER A WRECK

Anchoring uptide from a wreck and fishing baits into it is a far more complex method than downtiding. Many of the best charter skippers have earned their reputation for their ability to anchor consistently in a position where the anglers can fish the productive part of the wreck and not lose tackle from snagging in the superstructure. Anchoring is the tactic used to catch conger eels, ling, cod, whiting, dogfish, bream and wrasse. These species will not chase a lure, and prefer baits fished on the sea bed.

Once anchored, the angler needs to get his baited rig close enough to the wreck without snagging, not always easy in a very strong tide. Using the correct amount of lead and having a feel for the tackle as it is pushed downtide towards the wreck is an important skill. Because the line bows out in a loop in the tide when the lead hits bottom it is easy to think that the tackle is still drifting towards the wreck, when in fact it's the tidal pressure on the line pulling it off the spool. The technique is fully explained in the downtiding section, but basically, involves lifting the lead and allowing it to hop downtide, edging towards the wreck and the fish.

WRECK RIGS

When fishing from an anchored boat over or close to a wreck a standard downtide rig such as a flowing trace is preferred. In most cases this involves fishing for the bigger species, and so the strength of the rig is important, as is the single hook option – fewer hooks mean less chance of snagging. The flowing trace can involve a small sliding boom or simply the lead on a link sliding on the main line and stopped by a buffer bead and swivel. Simplicity is key to the success of a flowing trace. Even then, large baits may spin and twist as they fall to the sea bed, so take care to mount these to minimise this effect. A long rig boom will also help in deep water. Conger eels have teeth that can bite through light line, making a strong bite trace essential. This can be of plastic-coated steel wire, although most conger anglers nowadays use heavy monofilament line of 100lb-plus breaking strain with the hook fitted via a double metal crimp.

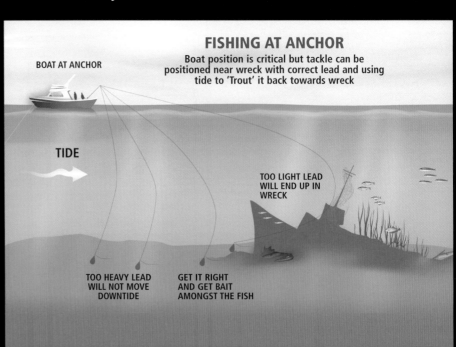

FISHING AT ANCHOR
Boat position is critical but tackle can be positioned near wreck with correct lead and using tide to 'Trout' it back towards wreck

BOAT AT ANCHOR

TIDE

TOO LIGHT LEAD WILL END UP IN WRECK

TOO HEAVY LEAD WILL NOT MOVE DOWNTIDE

GET IT RIGHT AND GET BAIT AMONGST THE FISH

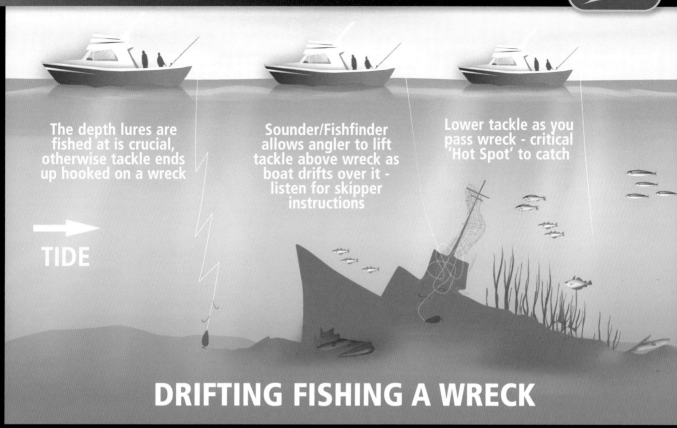

The depth lures are fished at is crucial, otherwise tackle ends up hooked on a wreck

Sounder/Fishfinder allows angler to lift tackle above wreck as boat drifts over it - listen for skipper instructions

Lower tackle as you pass wreck - critical 'Hot Spot' to catch

TIDE

DRIFTING FISHING A WRECK

GROUNDBAITING

This is a vital tactic for charter skippers fishing at anchor, especially near a wreck, because it can draw the bigger fish out of and away from their lairs. Some use specially made groundbait droppers, others simply chop bait and allow it to drift back downtide. One skipper I know uses a groundbaiting rod with a heavy lead to which a bag of bait is lowered and then turned inside out to spew its contents on to the seabed close to the wreck. A bonus is that conger eels away from the wreck are less difficult to land.

DRIFT FISHING A WRECK

Most summer wreck fishing is carried out on the drift. This catches most of the popular wreck species, which are taken on single lures like jellyworms and shads, multi rigs of feathered and artificial lures, or metal pirks. In all cases the fish targeted can be easily spooked if the boat is anchored permanently over the wreck and lures are continually dropped among them. However, because fish have short memories, motoring the boat uptide and drifting back over the wreck allows time for the fish to 'forget the lure that caught their mates.
The other advantage drifting has over anchoring is that the noise and scare

area caused by the boat's hull, the anchor rope and the anglers is absent, so the fish are not disturbed. The anglers can also target different areas of the wreck on each drift. In terms of fishing effort, drifting is far less tedious than having to anchor because if nothing is hooked, the boat either alters its drift or simply moves to the next wreck, without yards of anchor rope to retrieve.

On a modern charter boat electronic equipment allows the skipper to relay the position of the wreck and the fish to the anglers during the drift. An awareness of the variation in depth is vital in keeping valuable tackle away from the snags and putting the lures among fish. Anglers should always take notice of the skipper's instructions concerning depth. If he says reel 10 turns, reel 10 turns! You will not only lose less gear, but be in with a chance of a better catch.

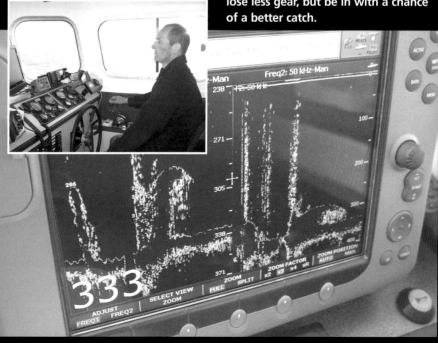

Listen for the skippers instructions to lift or drop tackle as the boat drifts over the wreck.

Are lures for catching fish or anglers? There are lots of different types and many don't look like any of the natural prey eaten by the fish. Golden rule never say never because some of the most eye shocking lures work!

JELLYWORMS, REDGILLS AND SHADS

A single lure on a long flowing trace is a favourite when drift fishing over wrecks and reefs, especially the inshore wrecks (within 12 miles of shore), simply because light tackle can be used to catch pollack, cod and bass.

The technique is to lower the lure close to the wreck and then retrieve it 15 to 30 turns of the reel handle, drop it back again and repeat. The speed of the retrieve is often important, and in many cases only one rod on the boat catches fish, often because that angler is retrieving at the ideal speed. It is important to retrieve steadily, occasionally speeding up the turns of the reel handle to give some variation.

The best rig for fishing a lure on a long trace involves a long boom, which prevents the lure tangling around the main line as it sinks to the wreck. Various types can be used, from the original French wire boom to the flying collar wire boom and the modern tubular plastic boom. All work efficiently.

TIP

■ If you get a bite on a lure deep, keep reeling! Species such as pollack and coalfish will follow the lure close to the surface, and so while the 30-turn rule is standard, fish can often be taken much higher up in the water.

JELLYWORM TIP
Add a head-hooked ragworm or a strip of mackerel to your lure to add scent when pollack are hard to tempt.

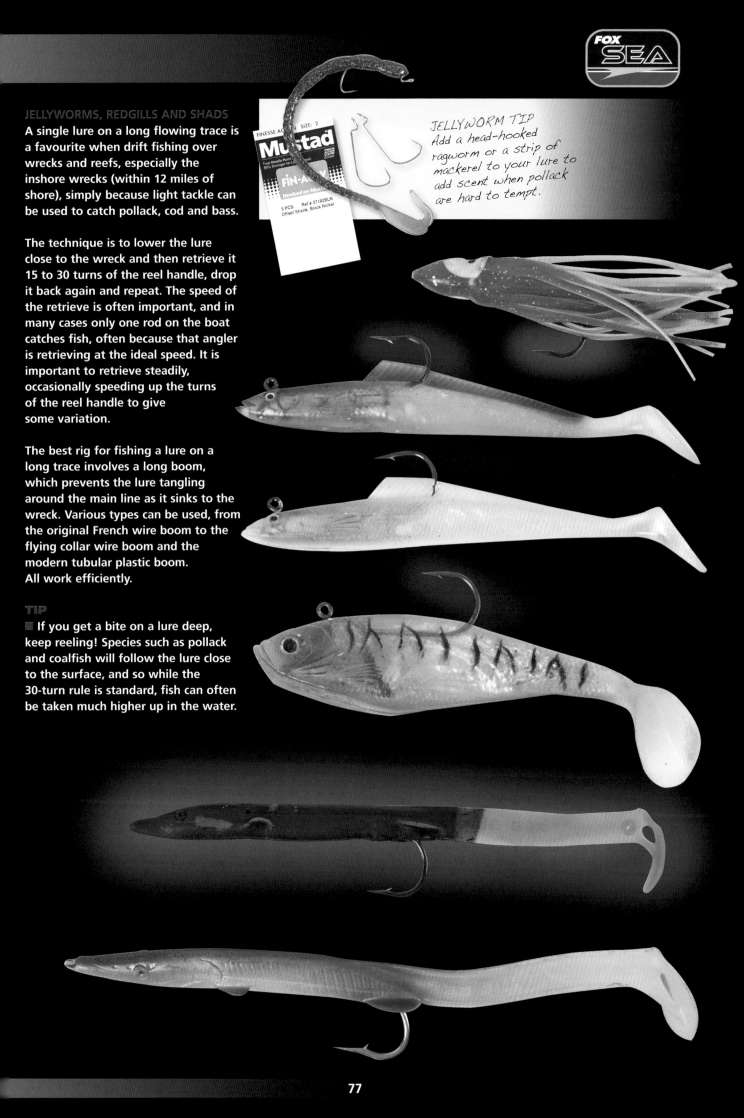

FEATHERS, LURES AND PIRKING

Pirking is most commonly used over the deeper wrecks and venues with a large number of species. The technique has a reputation for foul-hooking fish when they are in densely packed shoals around a wreck, and that's why it is also called 'ripping' or 'jigging'.

A heavy metal pirk, and sometimes up to four feathered or artificial lures above it, are presented monofilament paternoster style. The rig is fished sink and draw, with the pirk allowed to drop to the wreck with the rod lowered. The rod is then lifted as the reel is cranked. This allows the rig and lures to search the various depths, with the angler paying out or retrieving line to alter the position of the lures.

Pirking does carry a stigma among some boat anglers and skippers because of the foul-hooking tag, so in order to refine the tactic single hooks are often used on the pirk, with just one or two single lures fished paternoster style above.

Depth tip:

A depth counter is a handy aid to finding the depth the fish are at when lure fishing over a wreck. If you haven't got a depth counter, add a stop knot to the main line when you hook a fish so you can find that depth again. There are also a number of modern lines marked off in different colours to allow the angler to gauge depth accurately.

BAITED LURES

Baited feathers and lures are particularly productive in deep water, although their use is localised. The standard method is to fish a string of three to four lures such as Hokkais above a lead or a small pirk, and to bait each of the lure hooks with a sliver of mackerel or squid, sometimes even worms. The lures are then worked sink and draw as you would mackerel or cod feathers, although the action is slowed when a bite occurs to allow the fish to take the bait. The tactic is particularly effective on the drift and will catch cod, whiting, pouting, dabs, mackerel, haddock, gurnard and many other species.

WRECK FISHING TIPS

* Leads can often become snagged in the superstructure. An excellent tip is to attach your lead with a freezer bag tie or an elastic band, which will allow you to pull the rest of the rig free if it snags.

* Some modern tubular plastic booms have an anti-snag clip which allows the lead to be pulled free from the boom if it snags.

* When fishing with feathered lures use several, but cut the hook points off three to create a shoal effect. Lures that fizz and displace lots of water can be really effective on occasions.

If you get a bite on a lure deep, keep reeling! Species such as pollack and coalfish will follow the lure close to the surface, and so while the 30-turn rule is standard, fish can often be taken much higher up in the water.

POLLACK PREFER A LURE RETRIEVED STEADILY (NO JERKS)

REEL SLOWLY BUT STEADILY AT AN EVEN SPEED

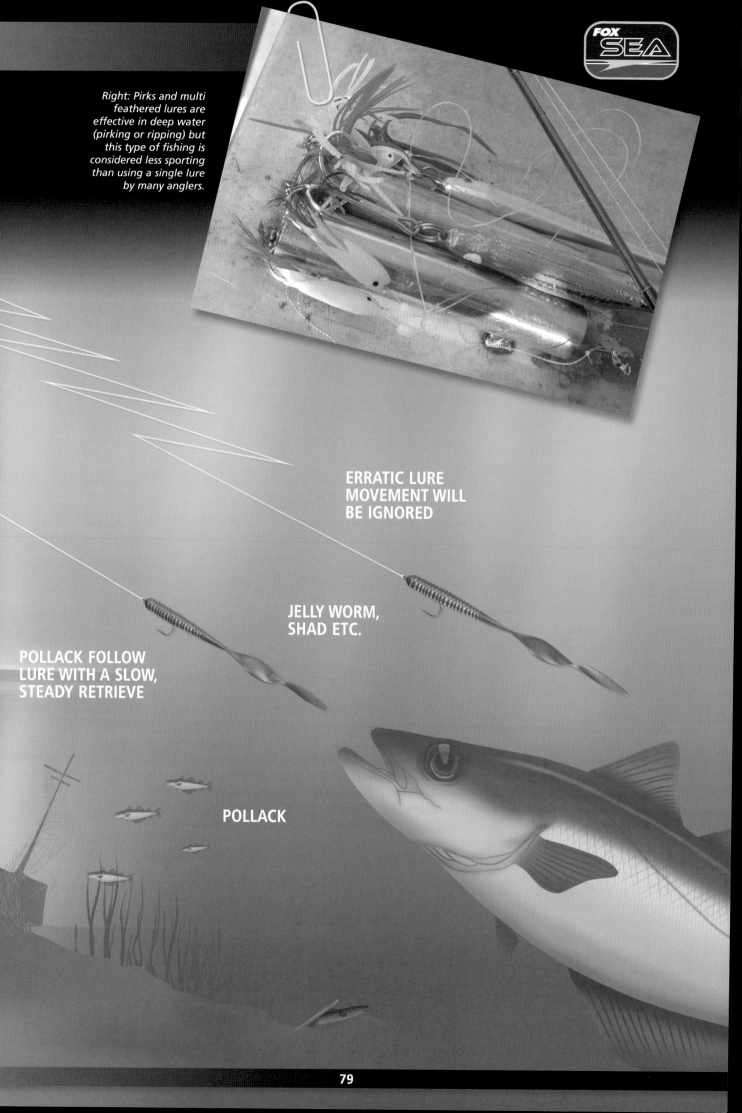

Right: Pirks and multi feathered lures are effective in deep water (pirking or ripping) but this type of fishing is considered less sporting than using a single lure by many anglers.

ERRATIC LURE MOVEMENT WILL BE IGNORED

JELLY WORM, SHAD ETC.

POLLACK FOLLOW LURE WITH A SLOW, STEADY RETRIEVE

POLLACK

Fishing with a small live fish as bait is effective for a variety of species, but most often for bass over a wreck with live launce, sandeel or joey mackerel. The method is the same as fishing a jellyworm or shad lure, with the sandeel lip-hooked on a long 10ft trace and allowed to meander slowly around the wreck as the boat drifts over it.

A bubble float can also be used in conjunction with a live sandeel when fishing from a small boat to cast or drift a bait some distance away – a technique used to catch bass in tide races and around rocks in shallow water.

Right: A live bait tank and air pump are essential to keep live baits alive, especially sandeels.

Below: The bigger the live bait the bigger the tank is required.

FISHING A BAITED SPOON

The principle of the baited spoon method is that the spoon is retrieved or drifted in the current, attracting fish to it, while the baited hook trails a few inches behind it. It's a bit like a seagull with a fish – other gulls follow in case the gull drops its catch. Usually the spoon is made of plastic or metal with a swivel attached. The short hooklength from the swivel can also include coloured beads and sequins to add to the lure's attractiveness. The spoon is fished on a flowing trace on light tackle, and is either cast and retrieved or presented on the drift.

The method is primarily for flatfish, although it will catch lots of other species, including codling and gurnards, in different regions around the UK. It is also particularly effective when crabs are active in estuaries, because the spoon and bait are kept on the move so the crabs are unable to strip the hook.

The response to a bite is either to stop the retrieve or, if drifting, to pay out line to give the fish a chance to take the bait.

■ There are no hard and fast rules about the colour or type of spoons, vanes and beads you use as fish attractors, but bait presentation can be enhanced by them.

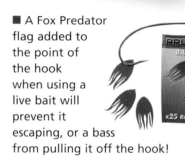

■ A Fox Predator flag added to the point of the hook when using a live bait will prevent it escaping, or a bass from pulling it off the hook!

■ A treble hook is great for live baiting, especially for bass, but if you want to return fish then it's important to flatten two of the barbs. The remaining barb keeps your live bait on the hook, while the flattened barbs will come out of the fish easily and not tangle in the landing net.

TROLLING

This method is mainly used for big-game fishing overseas and involves towing a lure in the wake of the boat, which in turn attracts some pelagic species which interpret the disturbed water as shoals of bait fish. In the UK, trolling is a viable tactic for catching bass inshore from the dinghy using lures like the Redgill and Eddystone eel. Make sure the reel drag is slackened off and the rod secure, and fish the lure 100 yards or more behind the boat. Trolling speed is critical, with 5 knots the optimum.

DOWNRIGGERS

Downriggers are a device used to troll a lure deep at a precise depth – a heavy lead is attached to a wire line on a winding device fitted to the stern of the boat, and this is lowered to the depth required. The line is then clipped to the lead, allowing the lure to stream out behind. When a fish takes the lure the line is automatically unclipped. This method is not often used around the UK, although it has some merit for species like pollack and coalfish.

Above: A tropical speedster caught on a trolled lure – note the Boga grip used to land and hold the fish without damaging it.

Trolling lures is a deadly tactic around the world for the mid water game species.

Receive all of this...

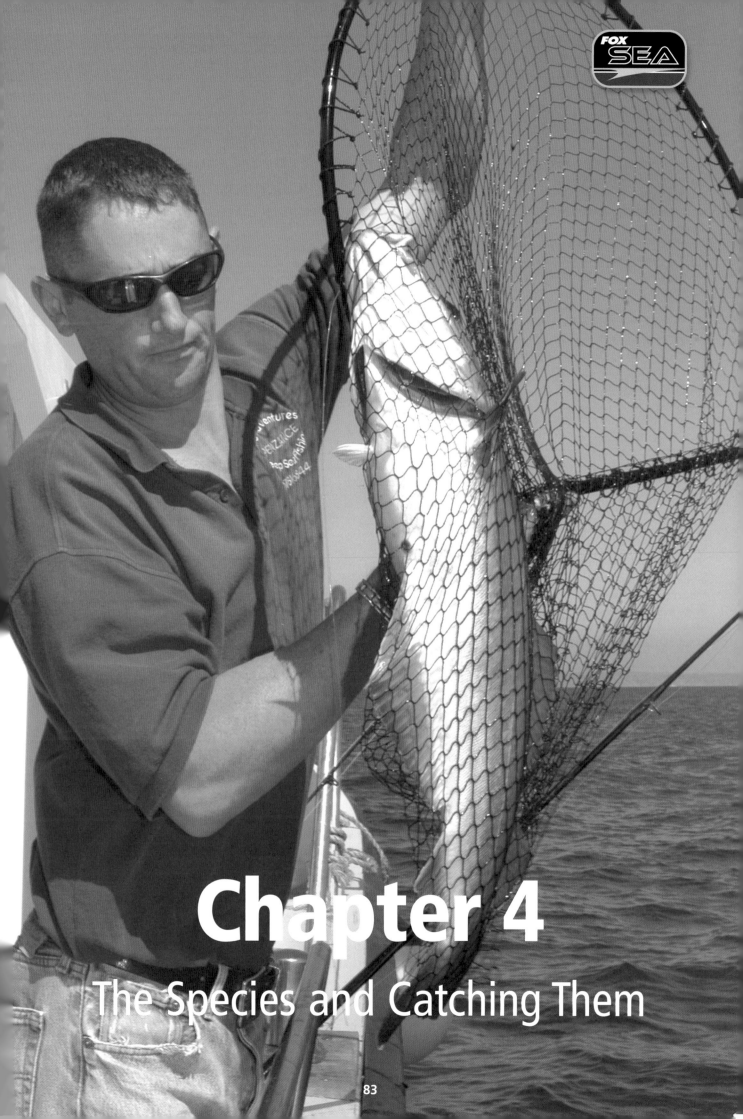

Chapter 4
The Species and Catching Them

If you gathered together all the species available to the UK boat angler and took an average size it would be under a kilogram. While the bigger fish are always the most popular angling target, the many smaller species are the bread and butter of the sport.

Most anglers set out to catch a big cod or conger eel, but on the way they will have to wade through the often unwanted dogfish, pouting, whiting and the like. To many any fish, any bite is what angling is all about, while to others catching individual large species is their goal. This always involves specialist tactics and hours of dedication.

Personally I enjoy catching any fish, no matter how small, and on occasions getting a bite is the best challenge of all – it is inevitable that sooner or later a specimen will come along.

So before we get down to the different species and the best way to approach catching them I would ask you to view all species with respect. Dogfish may be the scourge of the sea on when they grab baits aimed at the prime species, yet without dogfish the sea could be more barren than it otherwise is.

Not every day can be filled with monster fish or specimen catches, and hooking a few dogfish or pouting is an enjoyable alternative to catching nothing at all – remember that!

CONGER EEL (Conger conger)

The conger eel is the largest of the eel family and a true sea species, unlike its smaller cousin the silver eel, which ventures into fresh water. Unfortunately conger eels are not as common as they once were, and commercial box traps laid around the wrecks are said to be a major reason for the decrease in numbers. However, anglers must take some of the blame for continually

killing the largest breeding female conger eel on the wrecks around the UK. Fearsome ambush predators, the largest eels are mostly found around large wrecks or the heaviest rocky reefs where they feed on the smaller species. The British record may not reflect the biggest that eels grow. Larger fish have been caught commercially, but most conger anglers fish with tackle too light to haul them from their lairs, indeed

Above: The conger eel proves a tough adversary and a true test of tackle.

some of the real monsters may be too big to escape the wreck! The old school of charter skippers always believed that conger fishing was best during the slack neap tides, but nowadays some of the best catches are made during the strongest spring tides when, with modern navigation aids, boats can be anchored more accurately.

CATCHING CONGER EELS
Method: Fish for at anchor, legering large baits back in towards the wreck using a minimum 50lb class outfit for the largest eels.

Baits: Large cuttlefish and squid, whole mackerel or flappers, small pout and pollack.

Major UK venues: The ports in the South West and through the southern end of the English Channel are most prolific. Few conger eels are found in the North Sea.

Did you know?: Very large conger eels reside deep inside wrecks, and the usual tackle outfits (and indeed most anglers) are not capable of pulling the largest eels from their lairs. To break the British record will require 80lb-class tackle minimum!

Young conger eels are nicknamed 'straps' and can be distinguished from the silver eel by their slate grey colour, while the continuous fin around the body starts at the pectoral fin on the conger but near the vent on the silver eel.

CONGER TIPS
■ A strong hook length is favoured for wreck conger, and although their teeth are not as fearsome as those of a ling they can grind through light line quickly. What's more they can travel backwards, dragging line through the structure with predictable results! Few anglers use a wire hook length, traces being made from commercial grade monofilament (250lb breaking strain). This needs crimping to the swivel and hook because knotting is not possible in such large diameters.

■ Groundbaiting around a wreck really works. Some charter skippers use a bait dropper to tempt the bigger eels out and away from the wreck.

"Join the exclusive ton up club with a conger this big."

COD (Gadus morhua)

The cod family (Gadidae) is large, and includes many other common white fishes such as the pollack, coalfish, ling, whiting and pouting. However cod are the main target for most UK boat anglers, and although they are considered a winter species, in many regions it is possible to catch them all year around.

The cod's migration patterns see its major movement for spawning in the New Year, and in most regions its numbers inshore drop at this time. Rough winter weather also prevents the boats from reaching fish offshore.

Around the UK there are several populations of cod – the North Sea, English Channel and Irish Sea – and to a degree they overlap. However, the populations in each region do fluctuate, with heavy commercial fishing or a bad spawning year producing a cyclic effect on localised stocks. In general a cold winter favours cod because eggs

"John 'the cod' Wells with a 40lb plus cod."

(over three million per adult fish) and infant cod spend their first months on the surface and are easy prey to mackerel and herrings. Cold winter weather drives the prey fish south, resulting in a larger survival rate of cod eggs and fry.

Cod are a bottom feeding species, moving from the surface to the sea bed and starting life inshore where they feed on marine worms and crabs. At this stage they are described as codling or Tommy cod. Once they

Left: Big cod are great but this is the ideal size for eating.

reach breeding size (around 5lb to 7lb) the inshore diet cannot sustain them and they move to deeper water to feed on a diet of mainly fish. From then on they practically double their weight each year and reach spawning size in three or four years. This allows them to survive the usual setbacks.

Cod are widespread and are found in large shoals over all types of sea bed, including around wrecks and on sand bars, open ground and rough-ground reefs.

CATCHING COD
Methods: Main methods of fishing for cod are uptiding and downtiding from an anchored boat with a large bait hard on the sea bed, or fishing lures just off the bottom while the boat is drifting.

Above: A big pollack for Fox sponsored
skipper Paul Dyer of Brighton Diver.

POLLACK (Pollachius pollachius)

Despite being a close relative of the
cod, belonging to the Family Gadidae,
the Pollack (sometimes called lythe) is
a far more mobile predator that hunts
the water column between sea bed
and surface.

Look at the pollack's huge eyes and large
protruding mouth and you can see it's
built to catch live fish in the darkness
of the kelp forest, around wreck
superstructures, rocks and reefs.
Its power when hooked has given the
pollack more of a sporting reputation
with sea anglers, and because of the
demise of the cod in some regions
anglers, as well as the commercial
boats, have turned their attentions
to the species.

The pollack could soon become as
endangered as the cod, prompting many
charter skippers to return mosty of those
brought aboard. From a commercial
point of view the supermarkets label
pollack as 'white fish' and much effort is
made to suggest that pollack tastes as
good as cod. In truth, neither species
ever tasted that good – they are rather
bland compared to some others and only
popular because in the past they were
cheap and plentiful. ➤

Baits: Large whole cuttlefish are
recognised as a top bait for big cod,
while English and Calamari squid,
lugworms and fish baits also take
their share.

Lures: Where there are lots of cod
shoaling around a wreck they can
be caught on a combination rig of
pirks and feathers, while single
lure enthusiasts catch them on
jellyworms, Redgills, shads and
many other patterns.

Major UK venues: Cod are caught from
most UK ports, the bigger fish coming
from the English Channel, North Sea and
Bristol Channel regions.

Did you know?: It has been suggested
that if all the cod spawn hatched and
survived, the world would be knee-deep
in cod within 10 years. Three out of
three million eggs are thought to make
it to an inch long, which explains the cod
population's fluctuating fortunes

COD TIPS

■ Cod have bucket-sized mouths, and
the saying 'the bigger the bait, the
bigger the fish' really applies to them.
However, large baits can easily cover
hook points and result in missed bites,
and so if one species demands a
specialist rig it's the cod. A two hook
(6/0) Pennell rig is just perfect for fishing
large baits for this species

■ Often cod will be hunting among the
shoals of smaller whiting. A three hook
wire spreader will concentrate the
whiting around the rig, which in turn
will attract the cod.

Like the cod, the pollack spends its early years inshore around piers before moving to deep water and a fish diet as its size increases.

CATCHING POLLACK

Method: Pollack are most often fished for with lures, although they will sometimes take baits aimed at other species. Drifting the boat over a wreck or reef is essential when lure fishing for pollack because lures presented from an anchored boat will spook the fish. The successful technique is to fish a lure to the sea bed on a long trace and retrieve it at a smooth, steady speed. Pollack will also take feathers and pirks fished sink and draw, but not so readily. The terminal rig involves a long (French-type) boom to prevent the long trace from tangling. Trace length and diameter can be critical on some heavily fished marks. An alternative method is freeline a large head-hooked ragworm, and this can prove deadly over shallow inshore reefs.

Lures: Favourite pollack lures include old classics like the Redgill. The flame tail pattern was and still is a favourite. In recent years the Jellyworm and the various shads have taken over in the popularity stakes. Add a head-hooked ragworm or a long strip of mackerel to the lure to add scent – this is why a frozen sandeel can often catch more than the artificial.

Bait: Live sandeels can also be deadly for Pollack, freelined or with limited lead on light tackle over wrecks and the shallower inshore reefs. This is an enjoyable way to catch this sporting species.

Major UK venues: The bigger fish come from the deepest wrecks in the English Channel from ports like Dartmouth and Plymouth, while some potentially monster pollack and coalfish are taken from the deepest wrecks in the North Sea.

Did you know?: A supermarket thinks its customers are too embarrassed to ask for pollack and has renamed the species 'Colin'.

POLLACK TIPS

■ When lure fishing over a wreck for pollack take a couple of rods with different reels and line loads. This offers variety in the speed of the lure – pollack often prefer a lure retrieved slowly but positively.

BASS (Dicentrachus labrax)

The ultimate sport species in the UK, the bass is in a class of its own in terms of looks and habitat. It's a fish of the surface, surf and clear water and its sleek, spiky and silver image gives it a cult following.

The fact that it takes lures and is the closest to a tropical speedster that the UK has to offer adds to its attraction. In all probability more UK boat anglers seek cod than bass, and they probably catch more pouting and dogfish, but the bass is likely to be the first species given sport status once marine conservation here becomes law. Such a magnificent species deserves to be returned alive, so to be a true bass angler you need to be able to resist the urge to show your specimen around the local angling club or pub! Bass are not that powerful when

Pollack will take a mackerel sized lure as proved by this picture.

hooked and once on the surface they lose stamina quickly. However, that first flurry of spray and fins is a unique experience.

Bass are a very slow-growing species, with a 10lb fish said to be 20 years old.

Breeding maturity is not reached until six-plus years and this is one of the reasons the species remains under threat. Conservation areas like the Fleet in Hampshire have helped the smaller bass to increase in numbers.

CATCHING BASS

Methods: Downtiding or drift fishing. Bass are very much an inshore species, and although found around wrecks and reefs they do love to hug the shoreline, where they are an obvious target for the small-boat owner. Bass will take baits fished on the sea bed, as well as freelined lures and live baits. Baits: Bass will take whole squid, fresh mackerel fillets and heads, whole small joey mackerel, live smelts, pouting and scad, as well as live freelined sandeels.

Lures: Plugs, both poppers and divers and especially with a jointed action, are highly successful. So too are spinners (bar and Dexter Wedge types), Jellyworms, Slug-Go soft baits and artificial sandeels.

Major UK venues: Both shore and boat records for bass come from Kent, with the northern English Channel ports and lower North Sea (Thames Estuary) usually recognised as best for bass.

Did you know?: Small bass, called 'checkers' or 'schoolies', are common on some inshore venues, a pest and as boring as those small carp stocked in the carp puddles. Several double shots of school bass and you will understand why old-time angler Ian Gillespie, the man behind the Breakaway lead, once described a bass of 1lb as Heaven, but one every cast as angling Hell!

BASS TIPS

■ Handle bass with care – their dorsal fins are well known for being spiky but the edges of their gill covers are also razor sharp. Unhook small bass by holding them by the mouth to avoid spikes and gill covers (see left).

■ When fishing a live joey mackerel over a wreck the nearby presence of a bass is often given away by the bait's panic, which is transmitted to the rod tip.

■ Lots of rod and line boat anglers break the law around the UK by catching bass and selling them on the black market. To sell bass you need to be a licensed boat.

Alan Yates with a 9lb bass taken on a live sandeel aboard Mike William's Firefox out of Dover.

Above: Take care when handling. Bass are know for spikey fins and sharp gills covers.

LING (Molva molva)

The ling has an elongated body, pointed head and larger, sharper teeth than its close relative the cod. Coloration is grey to brown on the back and cream on the underside, with occasional black spots. Adult fish over 10lb are generally found only in deep water around reefs and wrecks although, as with the cod, smaller fish are caught from inshore rough ground marks. Ling are not the strongest of fighting fish size for size, and in common with the cod their numbers have been reduced by commercial fishing. Fish over 50lb are now very rare. Ling are capable of removing a whole mackerel hook bait in seconds without being hooked, especially during a slack tide.

CATCHING LING

Method: Downtiding or drift fishing. Tackle for fishing for ling with bait over the reefs can be as light as 15lb class, although over the deep-water wrecks 30lb is the normal choice, with 50lb preferred by those also targeting conger. The ling's sharp teeth can damage the hook snood, and so the larger diameter lines as used for conger are advised when targeting the larger specimens. Ling are also taken on pirks and lures, baited pirks fished on the drift being a tactic used to catch the bigger fish. Baited lures will also take the smaller ling from inshore wrecks.

Baits: At anchor, little is better for the largest ling than a fresh mackerel flapper, although they will also take small pollack or pout cut flapper-style. Squid and mackerel fillets or strips also account for fish regularly, as do baited feathers, muppets and Hokkais, but in general fresh bait is best.

Major UK venues: Western end of the English Channel and North Sea.

Did you know?: There are several species of small shore ling, called rockling. Others in the family include the rarer Torsk (Brosme brosme) and the very rare freshwater ling species, the burbot.

LING TIPS

■ Ling can be finicky feeders, and their ability to remove a hook bait in strong tide is legendary. Switching to a longer trace and lifting the bait off the bottom can entice them to take the bait more positively.

■ Ling have small but very sharp teeth, so watch your fingers when removing the hook or use a disgorger.

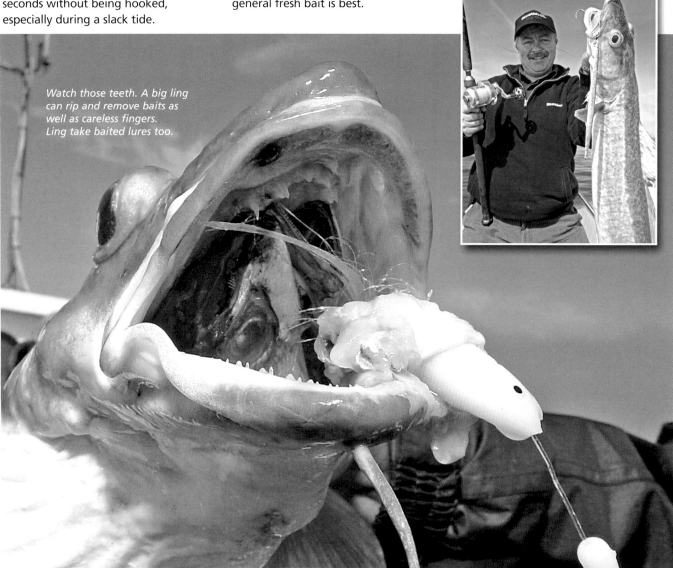

Big ling take lures and baited lures.

Watch those teeth. A big ling can rip and remove baits as well as careless fingers. Ling take baited lures too.

COALFISH (Pollachius virens)

A northern species of colder water, the coalfish, sometimes called 'saithe' or 'coley', is yet another member of the cod family and closely resembles the pollack in looks and habit. In the past the species was fairly common from the deepest offshore wrecks although now, to find the biggest specimens, you need to go far offshore into the northern North Sea or make a trip to the Norwegian fjords or Iceland, where the species is prolific. Tactics to catch them are similar to those for pollack and cod, although coalfish will accept a pirk of large lures more readily when there is great competition for food. They will also follow a lure up to the surface before taking it at the last minute.

CATCHING COALFISH

Method: Coalfish can be caught on lures from a drifting boat, several fished paternoster-style above a pirk being the favoured Norwegian method. They will take fish baits on the bottom, and sometimes the largest UK specimens fall to a large squid bait aimed at other species. Confusion between identification of the coalfish and pollack is easily sorted - the coalfish has a straight lateral line, that of the pollack is curved behind the gills.

Baits: Whole Calamari squid, cuttlefish, mackerel, and small fish – including other coalfish.

Lures: Pirks, Gummi Makks, shads, feathers and baited day glow lures.

Major UK venues: The deepest South West wrecks produce the occasional specimen, but the deepest North Sea is the UK stronghold of the largest coalfish

Did you know?: 'Coley' was the old-time description for coalfish sold in the fishmongers for the cat. Now, like pollack, it is often sold under the label 'white fish' or the latest supermarket con job, 'Colan'.

Perhaps the UK's most powerful fish, a coalfish.

RAYS
THORNBACK RAY (Raja clavata)
STING RAY (Dasyatis pastinaca)
BLONDE RAY (Raja brachyuran)

Several ray species are found around the UK including the stingray, blonde ray, undulate ray, cuckoo ray and painted ray – but the most common is the thornback ray. Rays are said to prefer a clear sand sea bed, although mixed hard ground can also be very productive, and sandy patches between rough ground or kelpie reefs can be productive. Thornbacks and stingrays are common in spring in many estuaries, where they feed on the peeling crabs.

Although the ray is a flat-bodied fish it is not technically a flatfish, but a member of the shark family. However, like the true flatfishes it leads a life close to the sea bed and tends to follow the bottom contours closely. That's why top venues for rays are often the deep drop-offs outside a sand bar or sand bank.

CATCHING RAYS
Methods: Uptiding and downtiding from an anchored boat.

Baits: Shellfish, crustaceans and small fish are the ray's main natural food, although they will take most of the angling baits during the season. Peeler crab is a front-runner in spring and summer, while fresh mackerel takes some beating on most venues. Other ray baits include frozen sandeel, fresh hermit crab, Calamari squid, lugworms and ragworms. Squid is often is preferred because when used in multiples it withstands the attacks of crabs and dogfish. Fresh herring and frozen Saury (Bluey) are also excellent baits, especially for thornback rays.

"Beware of the many sharp and abrasive thorns of the thornback ray"

Major UK venues: Thames estuary, English Channel, Solent, South West estuaries, Bristol Channel and the Irish Sea. The stingray is a mainly southern UK species.

Did you know?: The range and numbers of the blonde ray have increased in recent years, and it is far more common than it once was. The UK record is one of the most likely to be broken.

'Bluey' is the trade name for the Pacific Saury (Cololabis saira), a commercial food fish found in the North Pacific between Japan and the Gulf of Alaska and south to Mexico. It's a relative of the flying fish. As a hook bait it is soft, but extremely oily, hence its attractiveness to the many predators in UK waters that feed on mackerel. Recently the Bluey has been especially favoured for catching thornback rays.

RAY CATCHING TIPS

■ A long, hook snood is favoured by some ray anglers because this allows the fish to take the bait without encountering the lead or rig, especially uptiding, when a grip lead wire may spook a fish settling on it. A short snood will see the ray catching its nose on the body of the rig, which may scare it off.

A flower amongst the thorns – typical thornback ray often called Roker commercially.

■ Ray bites are generally a rod-bending run or a slack line, forcing you to pick the rod up and strike. Small pecks at the rod top indicate the ray settling on to the bait. Delay the strike until the fish moves off. Because of the way rays feed, dropping on to and cloaking the bait, they are sometimes foul-hooked in the nose.

■ Beware when handling rays of all kinds. They don't have teeth, but very powerful crushing plates and jaws.

Several of the family, like the thornback, are covered in sharp spines, both large and small. Watch out in particular when you hold a thornback by the nose – the small spines in this area can take your skin off! Many sea anglers hold a ray by the tail, but this is still spiny and may damage fish you intend to return alive.

Stingrays have a sharp venomous spine near the base of their tail which can penetrate a rubber boot, so beware.

TOPE (Galeorhinus galeus)

Britain's most popular small shark is highly regarded as a sport species. This is a fish whose numbers have risen as a result of the demise of some of the prime commercial species, and because anglers regard it as catch and release only – its numbers, average size and range have all increased. Tope are found in the largest estuaries as well as the open sea, and packs of small males are common on many venues. The largest pregnant females are found on a limited number of UK venues.

"Tope are the biggest of the UK's inshore sharks"

CATCHING TOPE

Method: Legering large baits downtide or uptide from an anchored boat. Tope can also be fished for shark-style with baits suspended under balloons and the addition of rubby dubby groundbait. This is mashed or minced mackerel, fish oil and bran introduced into the tide to form a slick.

Baits: A whole mackerel, or a flapper or fillet, is universally recognised as the all-round tope bait, but a live silver eel segment is superior. It deters dogfish (which can be a pest if you bait with mackerel fillet) and can be simply nicked on the hook for uptide casting. A smallish live mackerel (joey) is another bait worth using when the dogfish are taking baits aimed at tope.

Major UK venues: Thames Estuary, the Solent in Hampshire, South Wales, Lincs and Humber coast, and Luce Bay in Scotland.

Did you know?: Tagging tope is a popular part of catch and release. This being a large, tough species, lots of anglers and charter skippers tag and return all the tope they catch (right).

Tope bear up to 40 live young, the gestation period being around 10 months.

TOPE TIPS

■ A 6/0 hook is the standard for tope anglers, but many no longer use the two hook Pennell rig because of conservation issues surrounding unhooking. Circle hooks work fairly well for tope, and are well worth using if you are fishing catch and release for tope or any other sharks.

■ A rubbing leader is required for tope because, like the sharks, their abrasive skin and teeth can lead to a hooked fish damaging or cutting the line as it rolls. A 15-metre length of 50lb line is adequate.

■ Tope are sharks, and as such have extremely sharp teeth – handle with care. A medium-sized tope can be difficult to hold on to inside a rolling boat, with obvious dangers stemming from this. Grip the fish by the tail and pectoral fin (the fin nearest the gills).

■ The tope's teeth can bite through a mono hook length, so 30lb plastic-covered wire has long been the preferred hook length material – although more anglers now prefer single strand wire.

COMMON SMOOTHHOUND
(Mustelus mustelus)
STARRY SMOOTHHOUND
(Mustelus asterias)

The smoothhound is a member of the shark family, albeit a toothless mini member closely related to the rays. It has bony plates instead of teeth, which are used to crush its prey of shellfish and crustaceans. A smoothhound can be distinguished from the two other UK mini sharks it resembles (tope and spurdog) by its total lack of teeth. Smoothhound numbers have increased in recent years because the species is not commercially popular and anglers catch and release it. However, there is no room for complacency because it, like the tope, is increasingly being targeted as pet food! A fish of the largest estuaries, it is found relatively close to shore around reefs and banks of sand or mixed ground which usually hold a good head of crabs. The smoothhound is renowned for its fighting powers, and its initial run will test tackle and knots.

CATCHING SMOOTHHOUNDS

Method: Uptiding at anchor is the most usual tactic, although the fish are also caught downtiding. ➤

Tagging and returning tope is now a common procedure amongst many boat anglers.

Baits: Without doubt the best bait for smoothhounds is peeler or soft crabs, a big plus being that the crabs don't have to be in the most perfect 'peeling' condition. In many situations any crab will do as long as it's fresh and alive when put on the hook. In other words, hard crabs can be used because the smoothhound's tough jaws are capable of chomping on a bait most other summer species will refuse. However, quality peeler crabs still have a big advantage in that they can be peeled and mounted without the shell impeding the hook point. Peelers, especially those about to split open, also have far more fish-attracting juices than harder crabs.

Another popular smoothhound bait is the hermit crab, and many UK charter boat skippers prefer this small crustacean that lives in a whelk shell. It's biggest plus, of course, is that it is readily available and less expensive to collect and buy than the peeler. Many skippers simply toss a pre-baited whelk pot over the side on their way to a mark and pick it up for the next day's bait on their return. Hermits will keep alive overnight in a sack hung over the stern.

As the number of common shore crabs peeling dwindles, the hounds switch to spider crabs, then velvet swimmers or edibles. Between times they will pick up worm, squid and fish baits, so the rule is to fish with the bait that the fish are most likely to be looking for – in most cases this means prime peeler crabs!

"Catch, snap and release – it is considered very bad practice to kill smoothhounds."

Major UK venues: Smoothhound numbers have increased and their range has been extended. Strongholds include the Solent in Hampshire, the Bristol Channel, South Wales, Lincs and Humber Estuary.

Did you know?: Originally it was though that there was only one species of smoothhound, and that the fish with white flecks/stars on their flanks where immature specimens.

Now biologists tell us that common and starry smoothhounds are two distinct species. The difference is that the common smoothhound is viviparous and the starry smoothhound ovoviviparous. (Viviparous eggs hatch inside the mother and the young are born alive. Young fish hatching from ovoviparous eggs depend for a while on their yolk sac).

SMOOTHHOUND TIPS
■ Make sure your rod is safe and your reel drag loosened – a smoothhound can pull the rod in or break the line on its initial run.

■ Smoothhounds do not make good eating and in the main anglers tend to return them alive. It is frowned upon to kill hounds needlessly – remember, if you put your fish back, the next time you catch it it may be bigger.

■ Hang a large crab bait on the grip weight wire when casting uptide, or take a leaf out of the shore angler's book and use a bait clip.
The Breakaway Impact green head fixed-wire lead is ideal.

Smoothhound numbers and range has increased dramatically in recent years and they are now found all around the UK coast.

SHARKS
Blue Shark (Prionace glauca)
Porbeagle shark (Lamna nasus)
Thresher shark (Alopias vulpinius)
Mako shark (Isurus oxyrinchus)

It is possible to catch blue, porbeagle and thresher sharks from a number of UK venues. The mako is a rare, but not impossible quarry. The blue shark is the

Above: This big blue shark was landed aboard charter boat White Water out of Milford Haven. Possibly the best shark port in Britain.

most common, and with its indigo blue back and elegant pectoral fins it would win any beauty contest and stand apart from others in its family.

The thresher shark is less common than it once was. It gets its name from its long tail, which it thrashes about in a feeding frenzy on the surface when in pursuit of mackerel.

The porbeagle, also called the mackerel shark, is cobalt blue and sometimes confused with the mako, which some consider the most graceful and strongest-fighting shark of all.

CATCHING SHARKS
Method: In the UK anglers tend to fish surface baits like live mackerel via a balloon or polystyrene float, mostly on 30lb to 50lb stand-up gear with a rod harness. Overseas, larger sharks are sought with up to 100lb class gear and a fighting chair. To lure the fish to the boat, a rubby dubby/chum slick is leaked from the stern. This is a mix of fishmeal, bran and mashed mackerel, fresh or frozen.

Baits: Live mackerel is favourite, but a mackerel flapper, scad, herring or pollack can also be used.

Major UK venues: West Wales ports like Milford Haven, Looe and Mevigissey in Cornwall, or the Atlantic coast of Scotland.

Did you know?: Most famous of the world's shark anglers is American legend Milt Rosko. His book, The Complete Book of Shark Fishing, is a great read (ISBN 1 -058080-107-2).

There are more than 350 shark species found worldwide, but 75% of them are less than 5ft long. Sharks have been on planet Earth for 400 million years!

SHARK TIPS
■ Prepare your chum frozen inside a bucket and it will release its scent slowly over the day inside a net or perforated chum bucket dangled over the stern.

■ Single strand wire is the favoured hook length for catch and release shark fishing. It can be snipped close to the fish's mouth without the need to bring the shark onboard. ➤

*"Porbeagle and even mako sharks
are possible around the UK"*

SHARK FISHING ON THE DRIFT

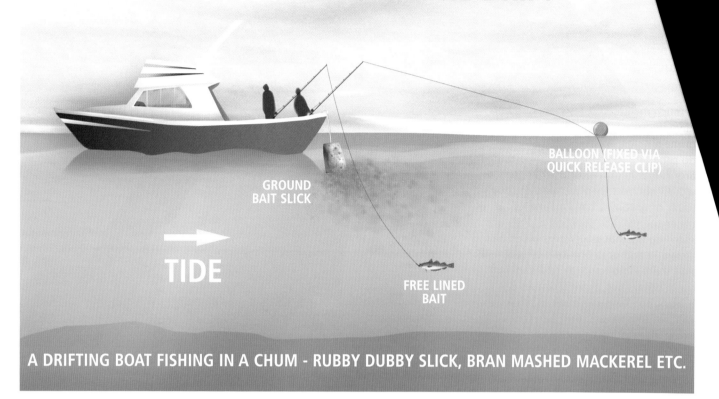

BALLOON (FIXED VIA QUICK RELEASE CLIP)

GROUND BAIT SLICK

TIDE

FREE LINED BAIT

A DRIFTING BOAT FISHING IN A CHUM - RUBBY DUBBY SLICK, BRAN MASHED MACKEREL ETC.

COMMON SKATE (Raja batis)
The largest of the ray/skate family, this is a fish of deep water, found in only a few locations around the UK.

CATCHING COMMON SKATE
Method: Fishing downtide from an anchored boat with 30lb to 50lb class gear with butt pad and harness. Reels are loaded with 45lb-plus BS line.

Baits: The best bait is a whole coalfish, cut flapper-style to increase the scent and blood trail. Large fresh mackerel baits are also deadly. A favourite is a whole mackerel baited on a 10/0 hook with an extra fillet added as a flapper to increase the blood and scent trail. Other baits include pollack and even dogfish.

Major UK venues: Orkney, Loch Lorn, Oban, Strathclyde and the west coast of Ireland.

Did you know?: Orkney is one of the most famous common skate grounds in the UK, with commercial fish of over 400lb landed.

SKATE TIPS
■ Common skate do not have teeth, just the bony crushing plates like the ray family, so there is no need to use a wire hook length – although their powerful jaws can easily damage light mono line. Commercial grade monofilament of 200lb, as used for conger eels, is more suitable.

■ A 4ft-plus flowing trace is commonly used to allow the fish to take the bait without running into the line and being spooked, but a much shorter hook length does allow bites to be spotted quickly and prevent fish being deeply hooked.

■ Skate explode into action when they near the surface and spot the sunlight, so be ready with the reel drag set for their sudden lunge back to the sea bed.

...FISH

Even Alan Yates has to put up with dogfish – this species is a pest when it takes baits aimed at other species.

...aligned fish whose numbers ...nefited from the demise of the ...species, lesser spotted dogfish ...rovide sport when little else is ...ound, although most boat anglers ...vould not miss them because of their habit of grabbing baits meant for other species. The problem is, they are shoaling bottom scavengers which will crowd in and grab any kind of bait, and there is no real way of avoiding them other than moving venues or making the bait and hook so big it will not catch them. Best bait for those attempting to choke off the dogfish is a large whole cuttlefish on an 8/0 hook.

Method: Uptiding or downtiding from an anchored boat with multi-hook rigs.

Baits: Marine worms, fish and squid. They show a preference for fresh baits.

Major UK venues: Most inshore boat marks – they are not so common in the North Sea.

Did you know?: In days past, the rough skin of the dogfish was used as sandpaper by fletchers for making arrows for English and Welsh longbow archers.

POUTING (Trisopterus luscus)

Of all the species in the UK seas, pouting, sometimes called 'bib' or 'pout whiting' are the most hated simply because, like dogfish, they take baits aimed at other species. Unfortunately, they are a fact of life and because they can reproduce in rapid numbers and are not commercially sought, their population is high. They are difficult to avoid from many marks, especially tinshore wrecks. Perhaps the reader needs to know little about how to catch them, although I would say that many of my angling skills were honed on pouting when I was young. There is no better practice for catching fish than catching fish! Pouting love all the marine worms, as well as shellfish, crab and fish baits. You can even catch them on baited lures over wrecks, indeed, the only way to avoid them entirely is not to fish!

Method: Downtide fishing with bait, or drift fishing baited lures and lures over wrecks.

Baits: All the regularly used sea baits.

Major UK venues: English Channel and Irish Sea (not so common the further north you go around the UK).

Did you know?: Pouting make excellent live baits for cod and bass. Fish them on a trace over a wreck if the first-choice baits, small mackerel or live sandeels, are not available

WHITING (Merlangius merlangus)

A small member of the cod family, numbers have multiplied inshore enormously in recent years with the demise of several of the commercially-sought species, including the cod. Aggressive towards bait and sometimes difficult to hook in slack water, whiting are prized only by competition anglers, and that's only because they are prolific and seem to have a need to grab a bait – any bait!

Method: Downtide with multi-hooked rigs including a wire spreader.

Baits: Fresh fish like mackerel, herrings, sprats, lugworms and squid. A cocktail of any two of these is often deadly.

Major UK venues: All around the UK, especially the English Channel, and the Irish and North Seas.

Did you know?: Whiting are one of the few cod family members that do not have a chin barbel.

WHITING TIPS
■ The wire spreader is an excellent terminal rig for whiting because its rigid wire frame prevents hooks tangling, while presenting three hook baits close to the sea bed.

■ Beware of the whiting's small teeth. After removing hooks, the small wounds their dentistry leaves can be extremely painful when bait juices enter them. OUCH!

HADDOCK
(Melanogrammus aeglefinus)

Another member of the cod family, the haddock is prized as an eating fish and consequently its numbers and average size have fallen in recent years. Its location is nowadays mainly the northern North Sea.

Method: Downtiding with b tackle or on lures, included b lures over deep-water wrecks

Baits: Worms, fish or squid, fea and baited Hokkais.

Major UK venues: They favour a northerly location, mainly in Scottish waters.

Did you know?: The haddock is easil recognised by the large black mark (thumbprint) behind the pectoral fin. The species is highly prized commercially, and as such has virtually been wiped out in UK waters.

Below: A personal best haddock for the author, Alan Yates.

bream species found in
which the most common
bream, which in recent
been an increase in numbers.
its popularity on the
plate may not help its
in the future. A sub-tropical
ies, the bream is found in small
populations in summer around
rock and weed reefs, with the bigger
fish tending to be found on the deeper
wrecks. Averaging 2lb, the bream is a
prize fighter and if fished for with
light gear it offers great sport. Bream
are considered extremely good eating.

Method: Light tackle – a mono
paternoster with size 2 hooks and
smaller trotted downtide to a rocky
reef or wreck.

Baits: Bream will eat almost anything
from worms to fish strips, with squid-
tipped ragworm and hermit tails
among the most prized hook baits.
Their ability to remove a bait from the
hook without getting caught is
legendary.

Major UK venues: The English Channe,
(peters out towards the North Sea),
Kingsmere rocks at Littlehampton,
West and North Wales and the
Channel Islands.

Did you know?: Other members of the
bream family that occasionally turn up
in the south-west approaches and the
English Channel include Spanish
bream, dentex, pagre, bogue, pandora
and, increasingly, the gilt head bream

– which has a localised population in
the Salcolmbe estuary reaching up the
Channel as far as Sussex.

BREAM FISHING TIPS

■ Keep baits neat and compact and
hooks small – bream have small
mouths and sharp teeth that can
whittle away large baits. A size 4 short
shank hook and a small cube of
mackerel or similar is the answer.

■ Beware – the bream has a spined
dorsal fin, not as sharp as that of a
bass, but still painful if it finds a finger.

GURNARD
TUB GURNARD (Trigla lucerna)
RED GURNARD (Aspitriggla cuculus)

The gurnards are bottom-dwellers with
a peculiar angular bony head and
bright coloration. There are several
species, the red and tub gurnard being
the most common. The largest is the
tub gurnard, which has blue edges to
its large pectoral fins, while the red is
all red and the grey gurnard – you've
guessed it – grey. Others include the
streaked gurnard. They are found on
offshore sand beds and clean bottoms,
and all will take a lure as well as static
baits. Bony, with spines, the species
should be handled with care. On the
plate they are something else!

Method: Downtiding with multi-hook
terminal rigs. Gurnards will also take
single lures like jellyworms and Redgills
aimed at pollack, cod or bass.

Baits: Worms mainly, but gurnards will
also take fish, squid and lures,
especially baited feathers.

Major UK venues: Mainly the southern
English Channel and Irish Sea.

Did you know?: Gurnards make a
grunting noise by contracting muscles
around their swim bladder.

Fish light for Black Bream.

"An armour plated head, front feelers and spines, the red gurnard is prized for its taste"

SILVER EEL (Anguilla anguilla)

The common or silver eel is a fish of inshore marks and estuaries. and unlike the conger it rarely grows bigger than 3lb at sea.

Method: Downtiding in estuaries with light tackle. Eels sometimes take spoons and bait aimed at flounders and plaice.

Bait: Worm and crab baits.

Major UK venues: River estuaries all around the UK.

Did you know?: The head segment of a 1lb-plus eel is just about the best bait for tope. Tough, it stays on the hook and is not eaten by pesky dogfish!

MULLET
THICK-LIPPED GREY
(Chelon labrosus)
THIN-LIPPED GOLDEN
(Liza aurata)

Three common species of mullet live around the UK, with the thick-lipped the largest, mainly found in estuaries and sheltered harbours. This is a fish that swims around boat moorings, where it provides sport on light coarse-style waggler float tackle.

Method: Light float or leger tackle.

Bait: Bread flake, crust or small harbour ragworms. Thin-lips can also be caught on a baited Mepps style spinner.

Major UK venues: Most of the large harbours and marinas, especially in the south and west.

Did you know?: The mullets among the largest and most widespread sea fish families.

MULLET FISHING TIP
Pre-bait the moorings regularly for a chance to catch this impressive species on light tackle.

...e British Isles in
...ckerel is a shoal fish
...rs in large numbers
...en feeding on the
...uch as whitebait. Watch
...Their range is affected by
...tures and the weather, so
...ernmost regions of the UK
...ce their mackerel season in mid
...e summer, whereas in the south
...outh west mackerel are around
...hore for most of the year, moving
shore and northwards in spring.

"Fresh mackerel is the bait that has caught more record fish than any other hook offering"

These are the most common bait fish used by boat anglers – the first step of a summer trip is invariably to catch mackerel for bait.

Method: Lures fished sink and draw from a drifting boat.

Bait: Originally a few chicken feathers tied to a hook were all you needed, and even a bare silver hook catches on occasions, although nowadays a whole range of more elaborate synthetic lures for mackerel are available.

They can also be caught on a smaller sliver of their own kind, fished on light float tackle or freelined in the tide.

Major UK venues: Mackerel are found all around the UK during summer, with the season longer in the south.

Did you know?: The mackerel is a close relative of the oceanic tunny (called tuna by the Americans) and bonito.

MACKEREL TIPS
■ A heavy lead is often the key to catching mackerel in deep water because it adds zip and fizz to the lures as they sink. A mistake many anglers make is to fish with a light lead (2oz to 4oz) in an effort to make feathering more sporting, but a light lead does not sink the lures very quickly so they lack the same animation going down as coming up!

SCAD (Trachurus trachurus)

This small mackerel species, sometimes called the horse mackerel, is much maligned because it is considered poor eating, although the flesh along its shoulder is tasty. It is not closely related to the true mackerel and is easily recognised by its large eyes and the row of sharp plate like scutes along its lateral line.

Method: Scad are caught on bait and lures from a drifting boat while fishing for mackerel. Small specimens of 3oz to 4oz make good live baits for big bass.

Bait: Mackerel lures and baited lures.

Major UK venues: Mainly the south and west English Channel and the Irish Sea.

Did you know?: The scad is a relative of the tropical amberjack.

WRASSE
BALLAN WRASSE (Labrus bergylta)
CUCKOO WRASSE (Labrus mixtus)

The wrasse is a fish of the coast and rough ground, although it does populate some offshore reefs.
There are several species but only the ballan and the brightly coloured cuckoo wrasse are considered worth angling for.

Method: At anchor, fishing downtide with multi-hook rigs.

Bait: Crabs and worms. Wrasse occasionally take small lures or fish baits.

Major UK venues: Rocky coasts all around the UK. Wrasse are not found in the silty estuaries and are rare in the North Sea below the Humber. The cuckoo wrasse is found mainly in the Irish Sea and off the south-west Irish coast.

Did you know?: All wrasse are born female and are slow growing. After a couple of years' spawning as females, some change sex to become males.

GARFISH (Belone belone)

Nicknamed 'green bones' or 'Mr Beaky' for obvious reasons, this species is only regarded as bait by many boat anglers – indeed, at some times of the year it is better than mackerel for catching everything from whiting to congers. Unfortunately it rarely tops 2lb. Garfish are great fun to catch on light float tackle on the surface during the slow times when you are after bottom fish.

Method: Light float-fishing or freelining from an anchored or drifting boat. Garfish are found within 12ft of the surface and are often seen jumping over flotsam.

Baits: A thin belly sliver of mackerel cut to resemble a sandeel, frozen sandeels or, best of all, a belly sliver of its own kind.

Major UK venues: Through the English Channel into the Irish and North Seas. It is less common in the north and has a preference for clear water, so avoids silty estuaries

Did you know?: The garfish is a member of the marlin family and is every bit as acrobatic – shame it does not grow to 50lb!

Steve Cole of Fox catches the bait (mackerel)

What a shame garfish don't exceed 2lb.

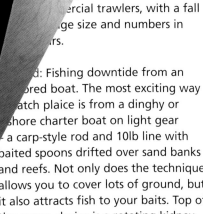

...sh, the plaice, easily ... pronounced vermillion ... suffered from the nets ...ercial trawlers, with a fall ... ...ge size and numbers in ...rs.

...d: Fishing downtide from an ...ored boat. The most exciting way ...atch plaice is from a dinghy or ...shore charter boat on light gear ... a carp-style rod and 10lb line with baited spoons drifted over sand banks and reefs. Not only does the technique allows you to cover lots of ground, but it also attracts fish to your baits. Top of the spoon choice is a rotating kidney spoon decked out with plenty of beads to make it rattle. Large broad standard tablespoons also work, but in my experience red and yellow sequins and beads are the hottest for plaice. The combination of light tackle and fishing on the move makes fishing for what is a small and less sporting species more enjoyable. Nevertheless, plaice use their arched bodies to deflect water, putting up a spirited 'fight' on light tackle.

Bait: Several baits are noted plaice-catchers, with ragworms tipped with squid strips or mackerel fished on a flowing trace a popular English Channel combination over sandbank venues like the Varne and Skerries Bank. Mussel is not a recognised plaice bait, despite these fish often being full of the tiny pea mussels.

Major UK venues: The English Channel sand banks like the Skerries, and inshore banks throughout the Solent.

Did you know?: A natrional decline in plaice average size and numbers has occurred nationally in recent times. Back in 1972 the British commercial plaice catch total amounted to 41,800 tons, worth

£7,997,000! Unfortunately this very slow-growing flatfish has finally succumbed to the trawlers, and fish in excess of 3lb are rare.

The minimum legal size limit for plaice is 27cm, the angling minimum is considered to be 28cm, but a more realistic limit is 30cm

The British record for the plaice is 10lb 3oz 8dr. Plaice are extremely slow-growing – a fish 24ins long can be as much as 20 years old.

PLAICE CATCHING TIPS
■ Early spring sees the plaice recovering from the rigours of spawning. Most are lean, hungry fish, so think twice before you bump a spent red spot on the head. Ask yourself thyis: is it sizeable, and is it good enough to eat? In particular, check the thickness of the fish along the sides. Spent fish are watery and flabby along the gut where the roe was located. It may be impressive to show others your catch but do you really want to kill a fish that you cannot eat? Carefully unhook and return it alive.

■ Plaice like sand patches between mussel beds and kelp, and this kind of mixed ground is less likely to have been trawled out.

■ Plaice feed in a leisurely manner – leave them to engulf the bait after pecking it about.

■ When drifting with a spoon, if you feel a bite, let out some line to allow the fish to take the bait.

Below: Bright red spots are a giveaway that this is a plaice.

TURBOT (Scophthalmus maximus)

One of the largest of the UK flatfish, turbot are sometimes confused with the smaller brill. They are found mainly on offshore sand banks in summer, surviving on a mainly fish diet, and that is the top bait to catch it. Turbot populations have been decimated by commercial nets in recent years and many marks no longer produce significant numbers of fish.

Method: Fish a flowing trace from an anchored or drifting boat.

Bait: Large fish baits such as fresh mackerel, herrings and sandeels.

UK major venues: The species was once common through the English Channel sand banks like the Skerries and Varne Bank at Dover, and today the largest concentrations are around the Channel Islands and throughout the south-west approaches of the English Channel and Irish Sea.

DAB (Limanda limanda)

The dab is one of the smallest flatfish, an inshore species mostly encountered by dinghy anglers. It has little angling prowess, but is highly regarded by many for its eating qualities. It can also be used as bait for tope. Found over clean sand and mud, it has a liking for marine worms and shellfish.

Method: At anchor using a wire spreadere or other multi-hooked terminal rigs.

Baits: All of the marine worms and shellfish. Dabs have a special liking for stale lugworms.

Turbot and brill can be con[...] both are caught from sir[...] sea beds.

Major UK venues: Found all around the UK, mainly inshore.

Did you know?: Reversed eyed (left-eyed) specimens are not uncommon. Tell a dab from a plaice by rubbing your finger along the skin behind the eyes. Its scales are rough – on a plaice the skin is smooth.

FLOUNDER (Platichthys flesus)

The most common flatfish around the UK, the flounder is a right side-eyed flattie and an inshore and estuary species, one for the dinghy angler. The largest specimens come from the south-west river estuaries.

Method: Downtiding from a dinghy, or casting and retrieving with a baited (flounder) spoon.

Baits: Peeler crabs, mud ragworms, small king ragworms and lugworms.

Major UK venues: Most estuaries, and sheltered beaches nearby.

FLOUNDER TIP
■ Tipping a worm or crab bait with a small sliver of fresh mackerel is a deadly cocktail in many estuary regions.

SPECIES TACTICS TIPS

FLOUNDERS, PLAICE AND DABS:
These species are top of the list when it comes to being inquisitive, and the first to follow something that glitters, moves or makes a noise. Small silver spoons, sequins, rattle beads, float beads and luminous beads all help catch these flatties.

Above: Plaice are suckers for attractors like beads and vanes in all colours.

COD, POLLACK, COALFISH, LING AND HADDOCK:
All these species will take lures, especially in deep water, and these include the largest metal pirks, feathers, muppets, shads and jellyworms fished either singularly or in threes. Much depends on the venue, depth of water and number of fish present, with a large head of fish likely to compete with each other. They will also take baited lures and feathers. Some fish not only grab a lure because they think it is food – sometimes they will attack something that invades their space. Most important to success when fishing with lures of any kind are depth and speed.

GURNARDS:
Will often take a lure aimed at other species, and can be caught on baited lures.

MACKEREL, SCAD, SANDEELS AND LAUNCE:
All will take paternoster-style rigs of feathers, and Sabiki-type mini lures are especially effective for catching these bait fish.

BASS:
The UK's ultimate lure species – catch them on surface poppers or diving plugs, Redgills, Bandits, shads and Slug-Go soft baits.

...used because ...ilar sandy

...n is an inshore fish ... by dinghy anglers. ...ens come from the ...t is considered a ...es.

...wntiding from an ...ue.

...arine worms, with lugworms ...gworms best.

...or UK venues: The English Channel ...d the Channel Islands.

HALIBUT
(Hippoglossus hippoglossus)

The largest of the flatfish, growing to over 600lb, halibut are now a very rare catch around the UK on rod and line. The species is farmed, fish being bred successfully in moveable cages in the sea lochs.

Method: Strong 50lb-class tackle fished at anchor.

Bait: Whole mackerel or other species.

Major UK venues: The species is no longer targeted in the UK and only the occasional specimen is landed from western Ireland, Scotland and the Orkneys. Alaska, Iceland and Norway are world venues that still produce fish regularly weighing more than 100lb.

Did you know?: The halibut, despite being a flatfish, feeds in midwater and is often caught in the Norwegian fjords on lures fished well off the sea bed.

Above: Surface plugs are deadly for bass.

TRIGGER FISH (Balistes capriscus)

Surprisingly aggressive, trigger fish are a product of global warming and in recent years numbers and range have increased well up the English Channel and Irish Sea. Watch your fingers, because the trigger is one of the very few fishes that will deliberately take a bite at you. There are lots of instances of divers having flippers and airlines nibbled at by the species – you have been warned! Found in rocky regions, they take crab and fish baits and swim in shoals.

SPURDOG (Squalus acanthias)

This species is less common nowadays because its flesh is said to be the best eating of the dogfish family. It is found all around the UK, but the largest concentrations are in the Scottish sea lochs. Caught on large fish baits and squid, it has teeth that can chomp through mono snoods.

RED MULLET (Mullus surmuletus)
An occasional visitor to the English Channel and Irish Sea regions, this fish

is also called the 'goat fish' and is prized as a food fish on the Continent. Not a member of the grey mullet family, it has its own Latin family name, Mullidae, hence the confusion. It is found on clean sand and will take worm and fish baits.

Right: A trigger fish and a red mullet are rarely seen together.

WEEVER
Lesser Weever (Echiichthys vipera)
Greater Weever (Trachinus draco)

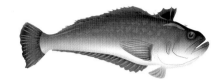

There are two species – the greater weever found in deep water and the lesser weaver inshore. Both have poisonous spines on the dorsal fin and gill cover which can cause considerable swelling and pain. No fatalities have been recorded in the UK from a weever sting although the venom is likened to that of a wasp, dangerous to the very young or old. A sting can be treated with hot water and bicarbonate of soda. Not sought deliberately, weevers will take most baits.

TOPKNOT (Zeugopterus punctatus)

This small flatfish is related to the sole and is most commonly found in rocky regions, rather than on sand. It is regarded as a mini species and has little angling value other than as a novelty catch.

LEMON SOLE (Microstimus kitt)

Not a true member of the sole family, this flatfish is related more closely to the dab and flounder – it has a very small mouth and that is the reason it is so rarely caught by sea anglers.

"If in doubt handle unknown fish with care because many species have sharp teeth, gill plates and many also have spines"

AnglingTimes

BRITAIN'S BIGGEST WEEKLY JUST GOT BETTER

Inside AT every Tuesday:

Hotspots of the week – the inform shore marks revealed

Venue focus – indepth tactical analysis of top marks plus tide times for when to fish them

Breaking news – the big stories first from the world of fishing

Round the regions – the local headlines and catches from venues near you

Your week – send us your catch pictures and win prizes – we guarantee to publish every photo

Latest tactics – 18 page section loaded with new bait and rig tips to help you get more bites

Tackle – see the latest gear before it hits the shops

Angling Lottery – 500 cash and tackle prizes every week

PLUS

UK MATCH MAGAZINE FREE EVERY LAST TUESDAY OF THE MONTH
UK CARP MAGAZINE FREE THE FIRST TUESDAY OF THE MONTH

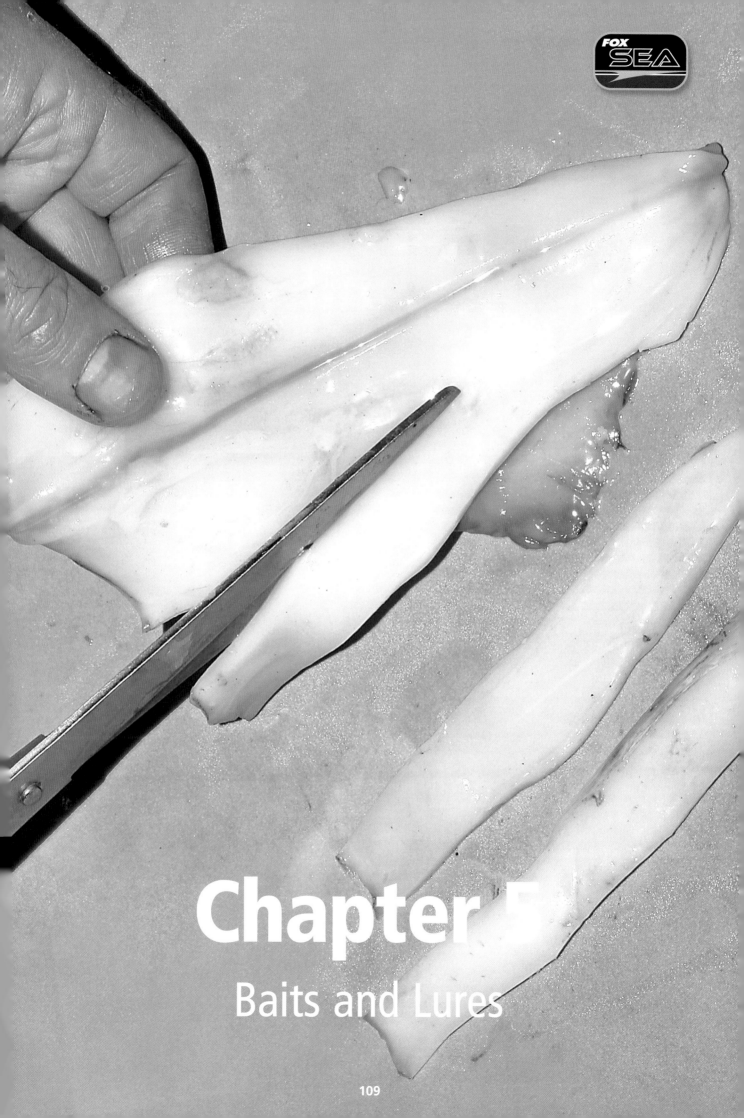

Chapter 5

Baits and Lures

FOX
SEA

Different species feed on different foods. Midwater fish may prefer small fish (lures) whilst bottom feeders will accept a range of dead baits.

Sometimes what you put on your hook is crucial to good results, while at other times the fish seem intent on eating anything. Large numbers of hungry fish feeding around a deep-water wreck may not give your offering a second look – to survive under competition they have to eat first and taste later. However, inshore on a flat, featureless sea bed a lone fish may have more time to be fussy. Fish seldom turn down a free meal, but they can be tuned in to a particular food supply.

Tunnel vision towards a single food source is very often to blame for a lack of response to your hookbait, and many species look for a specific food in a particular place or at a specific time of year. For instance, a whole squid fished on the sea bed may be ignored by bass up off the bottom chasing sandeels and mackerel, and the same applies to cod chasing small fish and not looking for a lugworm. Smoothhounds may be hunting peeling crabs, ignoring all other baits.

Most sea anglers rely on just three of four major baits – a lugworm and squid combination in winter, fresh mackerel, whole squid, cuttlefish, worms and live fish in summer.

Everyone should try to obtain the bait of the day or the season. The right bait is a great leveller for those with limited skills.

MACKEREL

Fresh mackerel is one of boat angling's most successful all-round baits, particularly in summer when large shoals of the species are all around the UK coast. Mackerel flesh has accounted for many UK and Irish records simply because it's a plentiful species that many of the larger predators chase, and it is readily available to anglers.

Mackerel flesh is extremely oily, with a potent scent. The blood content is also high, and these two attributes add to its attraction. Mackerel is best used fresh: with age the flesh becomes softer and less attractive to predatory fish. It can be used frozen when fresh mackerel is not available, and still accounts for lots of species, but freezing softens the flesh even more.

During summer the first task on any boat is to catch the bait on the way to the mark, and a fish box can easily be filled with mackerel taken on six feathers or similar lures fished sink and draw on the drift. Use the smallest feathers and lures because these also catch launce, herrings,

scad and the smallest joey mackerel, which are superb both as live and cut bait.

OTHER FISH BAITS

A number of other oily fish are used as bait, particularly fresh herrings in autumn and winter. Some small boats carry a small drift net to catch them. Herring is excellent fished in strips or cutlets for whiting, and is considered exceptional in some regions for winter thornback rays. Sprats too make the ideal small bait and are most commonly used in winter for whiting, cod and dabs.

SILVER EEL SEGMENT

A short 6ins-plus segment of a fresh live silver eel is an excellent summer tope bait, particularly the live head end. Eel skin is tough, and a 6/0 hook nicked into it will hold for uptide casting. Silver eel segments are not pestered by dogfish, whereas a mackerel filet will attract them from miles around. A few giant bass fall to silver eel baits every summer.

Below: Fresh mackerel is a versatile bait for many bottom species and can be used in strips, fillets, while or head and guts (flapper).

"Small bass are suckers for small feathers or tinsel lures. Adult fish are not so easily fooled."

Bass are the number one predator that can be targeted deliberately with a small live fish. Launce and sandeels can be deadly for bass, as well as most other species from pouting to thornback rays. Fished on the drift using a long light flowing trace, the launce is simply hooked through the lip and trailed past a wreck (add a Fox Predator bait flag to the hook point to prevent the eel escaping or being pulled off).

Small joey mackerel also make the ideal live bait for bass, while in deeper water they catch ling, conger and tope.

Less successful live baits include scad, smelts, small pouting, poor cod and small pollack. Every boat should have a live bait well, and increasingly charter skippers and private boat owners are installing a water-pumped tank for keeping bait fish alive.

Live sandeel is deadly for bass, pollack and some other species. Here Sea Angler magazine editor Mel Russ shows his way of fishing a live sandeel.

LIVE BAIT TIPS

* Whatever live bait you are using (and this includes fish or prawns), hook it on the hook so that it remains active – through the lip, tail or back, not vital areas like the head or belly.

* For small live baits like sandeels avoid using large heavy hooks that will drag the fish down and drown them as they fight to keep swimming. Special lightweight bass live bait hooks include the Fox Power Point BYH range.

SQUID

The squid is a 10-tentacled member of the Cephalopod family which includes over 300 different species. The scientific name comes from the Greek and means 'feet coming out of head', and if that is not odd enough, the creature is jet propelled. It can swim backwards at 20mph by forcing water through its siphon. The prey of marine species from sperm whale to mackerel, it is also a highly sought-after human food as well as a fishing bait.

The most commonly available type of squid in the UK is the Calamari, a small species from the Pacific coasts of California and Mexico. In recent years the pressure on it as a food item has seen shortages, and now other so-called 'Calamari' are coming in from elsewhere. These include the smaller Liligo squids from Japan, which are more like mini-cuttlefish and are most effective for inshore fishing.

The larger English squid, sometimes available fresh from your local fishmonger or market stall, is a tougher, thicker bait, best cut into small chunks or strips before freezing. The third most common squid is the cuttlefish, from the same family but with a broader, flatter back and the famous cuttlefish bone beloved of cage birds. Again it is available fresh or frozen – in terms of its fish-catching properties it seems to make little difference which.

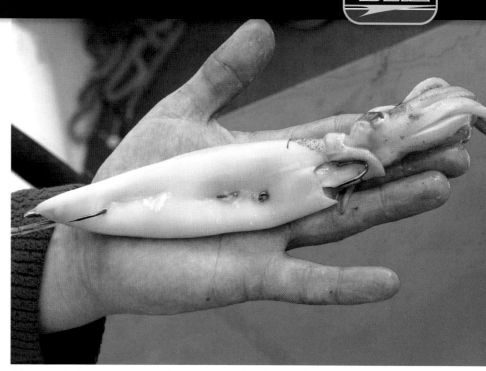

Above: A whole Calamari squid is favoured big fish bait in the UK.

The Calamari is a versatile one-hook bait for big fish inshore and general boat angling, especially for winter codling. It also catches bass, dogfish, conger eels and rays, while cut into strips and slivers and cocktailed with lugworms it is just about the most commonly used bait for all-round dinghy fishing. Calamari is cheap and always available from tackle dealers, or you can buy a bulk box from the supermarket.

English squid is less easily found, and being bigger and thicker than the Calamari it is best fished in strips in squid/worm cocktails for cod, whiting, pollack and plaice. The head alone is a popular bait for conger eels and ling.

Cuttlefish are a great bait over wrecks for

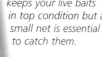

Left: A live bait tank keeps your live baits in top condition but a small net is essential to catch them.

conger eels, ling and cod in regions where dogfish can remove a single or multi Calamari hook bait quickly. Cut out the cuttlebone and mount the whole cuttlefish on an 8/0 hook for the bigger species.

The smaller Liligo squid are ideal for freelining, floatfishing for bass and pollack, and inshore dinghy fishing for cod.

Fresh frozen squid catches best, and because it's relatively cheap this means that once thawed it should not be returned to the freezer for use again!

It is essential when using a whole or large squid or cuttlefish that the hook is big enough not to be masked by the bait. To stop it slipping around the hook bend and blocking off the point it should be secured – this makes the two-hook Pennell rig the perfect configuration for really big squid baits, which can be tied on with elastic cotton for added security.

You can improve the attraction of your squid bait by removing the skin, while if cutting it into strips, first clean the inside and remove the 'plastic' skeleton. The head and legs can also be used whole, or as a tipping bait. ➤

SQUID BAITING TIPS

* Buy your squid from the supermarket in 1/6 or larger boxes. The advantage of this is that, by law, it will be in good enough condition to eat. A tackle dealer buys in bulk, thaws out and bags squid in smaller numbers and sometimes this can lead to bait deterioration! You can do the same more carefully and ensure quality squid and better value for money. Club members grouping together can buy in a winter's supply very cheaply direct from the fish market or fish importer.

* The skin of squid is always discoloured with a slight tinge of pink or black. Peel it off by tearing the two fins at the top of the mantle downwards, banana style, to leave a clean white bait. Squid that is bright pink is 'off', so discard it.

* Squid and cuttlefish are caught commercially on jigs. These oddly-shaped multi-hook lures appear in some tackle shops.

* One of the best ways to bait with squid during the winter is to tip off a lugworm with a tapered, diamond-shaped strip - a favourite for cod, whiting and other species. You can make the squid even more attractive by cutting 'legs' into the strip with scissors after baiting up.

* It is important to cocktail squid to lugworm in the correct ratio. A pencil-sized strip is ideal for most small fish using a size 1/0 hook, the head of a Calamari is perfect for cod on a 3/0-plus hook, but beware of overdoing the size of a strip or head section so that it masks the hook point!

HERMIT CRABS

Hermit crabs are small crustaceans that live in discarded whelk shells. It is the very soft abdomen that is especially attractive as bait. They live on rough ground with a mix of small rocks, and in some regions such venues form hot marks for smoothhounds. This is when the bait is particularly deadly. At other times the abdomen will be irresistible to rays, bream, dogfish and pout from inshore marks.

Lots of charters skippers lay pots for hermit crabs and pick them up and re-bait them on the way to a fishing mark. Hermits cannot be kept alive for long out of water and an aeration system is needed if they are to stay alive in water. Hang a sack or a purpose-made wooden box over the stern at the mooring to keep you hermits in good fettle. You will require lightweight bait elastic to secure hermit crab baits on the hook, especially multiples.

SHELLFISH

Shellfish baits including mussels and razorfish are often preferred in a smelly state. This is because after being

Above: Large yellowtail lugworm are considered the best of the worm baits.

HERMIT CRABS TIPS

* To remove hermit crabs from their shells without making a mess on the boat by breaking them, place a few in a shallow bucket of water as you leave harbour. Avoid keeping a lot together, as they fight like gladiators!

* Just like peeler crabs, once dead hermit crabs lose their attraction. An hour after giving up the ghost they are next to useless!

* The worm sometimes found in the shell behind the crab is itself a worthwhile bait for small inshore species.

* Did you know that the reason the hermit crab's right pincer is always larger is because it seals the hole inside the whelk shell when the crab retreats into it?

killed en masse by a storm they may be buried for a week and then exhumed by a big sea, when the fish home in on their strong scent. They are not a front line offering but can be used effectively for cocktailing or bulking up a bait, especially inshore.

LUGWORM

Lugworm is the commonest bait simply because it's widely available from tackle dealers and is relatively easy to dig around much of the coast. It is not, hoever, the best bait, an accolade that would have to go to mackerel or even squid.

The fact that lugworm can be threaded on the hook easily not only makes it simple to use but efficient in terms of hooking fish. For boat angling, worms tend to be an inshore and estuary bait, especially in summer when offshore the larger fish baits and squid are more effective. In winter lugworm does come into its own for cod, although in regions infested with dogfish squid is more effective, and to many anglers cuttlefish, when available, remains the best bait of all for big cod.

The largest, toughest black or yellowtail lugworms are worth two of the common kind. They are not widely available, because they can only be

dug during spring low tides. However, the tactic with lugworms of both kinds is to make a decent-sized bait that should be replaced every cast, because the worms soon shrink and lose their scent.

RAGWORM

Ragworms score highly on scent and movement. Several inshore species will respond to the wriggling tails of a ragworm, and fishing whole one head-hooked, so that it 'swims', is a deadly way to target pollack. Ragworms are regional, most generally available around the largest estuaries, and this is where they prove the most effective. Plaice and flounders respond well to ragworm fished on the drift teamed with a lure or a spoon.

Above and right: Hermit crab deadly for smoothhound.

WORM BAITING TIPS

* Using a baiting needles for large multiples of lugworm and ragworm ensures that the hook goes through the centre of the worm. You will need a fine, sharp needle for ragworms, while blunter needles are better for lugworms.

* Store your worms in dry newspaper inside a cool bag/box and don't lay out the entire supply in the sun - keep some back for later in the day and they will stay in good condition. Live yellowtail lugworms stored in water can deteriorate if they get warm, so add a cool pack to their bucket to keep the water temperature down.

* Ragworms have pincers, and the big specimens can give you a nip. Cut the heads off with scissors before baiting if you are concerned.

* Beware - the juices of ragworms and peeler crabs can be painful if they get into cuts on your hands.

Left: Lugworm cocktailed with a strip of fish or squid is ideal for the small species and match fishing.

Many sea anglers fail because they abuse their bait. Fresh bait left out in the elements, especially wind and rain, can be ruined in minutes and more than one angler has wrecked his chances of a catch by simply throwing his bait into the back of the car on a sunny day, only to find it has turned into a hot mush on arrival. Beware, too, of laying too much bait out in the sun and spray. Even fresh mackerel, filleted and left on the bait cutting board too long, can be ruined in this way. So only unpack or cut up the bait as you need it. Use a cool box or bag to store the remainder – it will double up to keep your catch fresh on your journey home.

FROZEN BAITS

Frozen bait is only as good as it was when first frozen, and bad management can often wreck its effectiveness. Even the best known and most consistent commercially frozen baits, once in the hands of a dealer (or charter skipper) can be ruined because some people are not that fussy about the way they store and handle them. The time lapse between delivery and the bait going into the freezer, the way it is packed and the efficiency of the freezer itself all have a bearing on its quality, and frozen bait can only deteriorate.

The fact is that most frozen baits look okay in that state, and it is only when they are thawed that you discover the awful truth! The worst-case scenario I have come across is a guy who displayed samples of his frozen baits outside the

Below: Blast frozen sandeels are easily kept in the freezer. The best are Ammo and Baitbox.

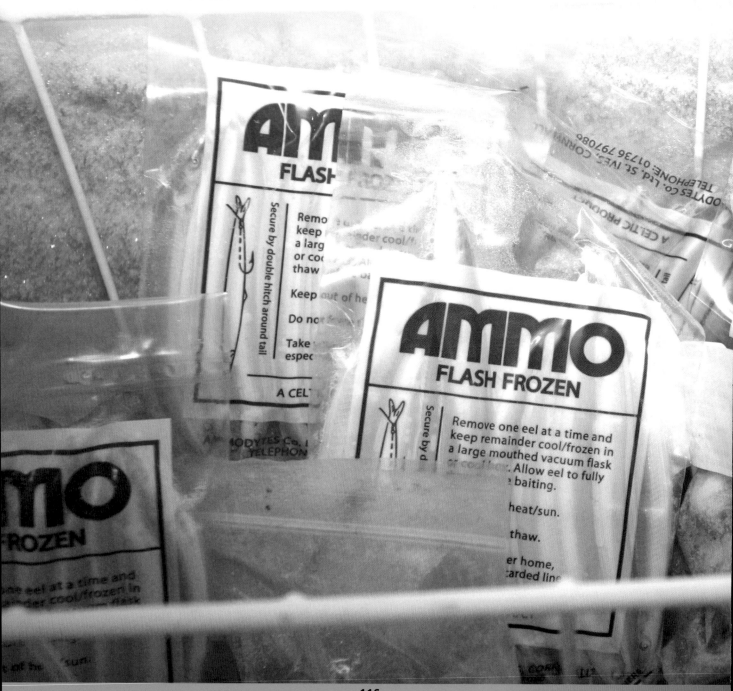

freezer and then re-froze them overnight! So, when buying frozen baits,

"Remember, frozen baits don't get any better with age!"

find a dealer with a reputation for looking after them. If his fresh bait is good, it's likely his frozen bait will be too. Remember, too, that lots of tackle dealers freeze their own bait. This is no

BUYING TIPS

* Collect your frozen bait from the dealer and transport them in a cool bag or box with a freezer pack, this is especially important in summer and during a long session in sunshine. Frozen bait can go off just the same as fresh.
* Only remove what you need from the cooler as you fish. A tip is to place pre-baited hooks inside the cool bag.
* A busy tackle shop will see its frozen baits turned around rapidly. Being sold out is a sign that next time bait is in stock it will be a fresh consignment!
* A freezer cabinet in need of defrosting is a sure sign of frozen bait abuse - avoid. If it looks as good as the supermarket you are on a winner!
* Look for clean looking, ice-free packets - baits take on a white or brown freezer burn when they have been thawed and then re-frozen.
* Squid has a pink skin, but the flesh goes bright pink when thawed and refrozen. Look for pure white flesh.
* Crabs that were dead when frozen look black. Black in cuttlefish is the ink.
* Avoid frozen sandeels and mackerel that have bloody heads or are discoloured inside the packs

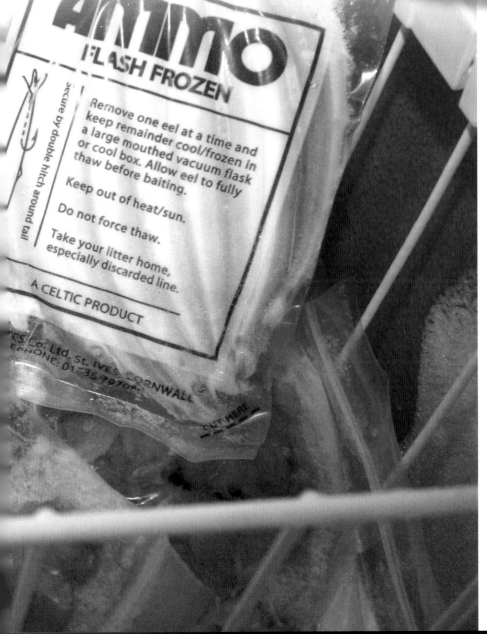

guarantee of quality, so check the freezer contents closely.

THE FAVOURITE FROZEN SEA BAITS

BLUEY: One bait that has caused lots of confusion and interest among UK sea anglers recently is the Bluey. This frozen fish bait, a recent addition to the bait cabinet, is the Pacific Saury (Cololabis saira), a commercial food fish found in the North Pacific between Japan and the Gulf of Alaska and south to Mexico. It is caught near the surface using bright lights and it's a relative of the flying fish, also called the mackerel pike. As a hook bait it is soft but extremely oily, hence its attractiveness to many predators in UK waters that feed on mackerel.

The Bluey is especially effective for thornback rays and is a great alternative when mackerel are scarce.

MACKEREL: This is the easiest fish bait to freeze yourself, but you must catch it fresh and gut or fillet it immediately to prevent the flesh going soft. The quality of frozen mackerel varies according to the seasons and what it has been eating. The oiliest fish of midsummer that have been feasting on whitebait are often softer than the early-season fish. Freeze singly as quickly as you can. The commercially blast-frozen
mackerel, either whole or in fillets, takes some beating. ➤

SANDEELS: The quality of the commercial blast-frozen sandeels can rarely be bettered, but it is essential to keep the eels frozen right up to the time they are mounted on the hook. Use a small stainless vacuum flask to get the best from your sandeels, and discard any that are soft or have burst bellies.

RAZORFISH:
Some anglers say this bait is best blanched prior to freezing but, as with most shellfish, the texture of the flesh does soften with freezing, making it more difficult to keep on the hook. Bait elastic is essential. Mixing razorfish in a cocktail with another bait like lugworm or squid is a classic way to get the best from it.

SQUID: You can buy a box of Calamari squid from the supermarket – part thaw and then bag up in threes. Calamari is the frontline frozen bait and as such is much abused. Take just what you need for each fishing trip rather than re-freeze what you have over. Cuttlefish are also available frozen and have a good reputation as a big-fish bait.

PEELER CRAB: This is not a frontline boat bait but it beats everything else, including hermit crabs, for summer smoothhounds. It needs to be in the prime state of peeling when frozen, which is not always commercially viable, so freezing your own is the best option. Use only live crabs that are about to shed, and remove all their shells before wrapping in foil and freezing rapidly.

FREEZING YOUR OWN
Most anglers will have tried freezing their own bait at some stage, although often it is leftover bait that has already been thawed and left in the sun. This is a big mistake, with the notable exception of some shellfish, like clams, which actually improve as they start to go off. The golden rule is to freeze only the freshest bait, wrap it individually in clingfilm or foil and freeze as quickly as possible in a plastic bag. An aluminium or steel tray in the freezer is said to be the most rapid way to freeze small baits. DIY vacuum packing is also now possible, and this is the complete answer

to freezing your own baits. A quality freezer is essential, and even then, keep an eye on how long items have been frozen. Bait will not be as good after six months in the freezer as it was when three weeks old. Label your bait with contents and date frozen, and that way you can rotate supplies.

Above: Calamari squid can be purchased in 1lb or 7lb boxes from the supermarket etc and is one of the most economical baits.

Below and roght: Baitbox has a quality range of frozen baits.

BAITBOX

Chapter 5 Baits and Lures *Presentation*

Bait presentation is more important in terms of ensuring the fish is hooked t than convincing them the bait is natural. Fish are not aware of hooks or line, and even with catch and release it is unlikely that fish would be caught and returned often enough to wise up like their freshwater cousins. So hiding the hook from the fish is not a priority, but ensuring that it does its job is.

Most baits presented on the hook in the boat before being lowered into the sea look perfect. But before they hit the sea bed several things conspire to ruin presentation. For example, a bait dropping through deep water will spin and lose its shape and scent or blood, so the first essential is to mount it so that it will remain relatively intact until it reaches the bottom.

Matching the hook size to the bait is a priority. A small hook in a large bait will be lost, reducing the chances of a strike finding the fish's mouth. A small bait on a large hook is less problematic, although you may miss out on hooking smaller fish, but bear in mind that a stingy bait will lack scent and staying power.

Sloppiness can allow the bait to fall or be pulled around the bend of the hook as it sinks, masking the hook point totally, so take extra effort to secure the bait by passing or twisting the hook through it, or tying in on with elastic cotton.

"A big bait catches big fish."

SPECIES BAIT PREFERENCES

Cod: Despite having big bucket mouths cod prefer fresh baits, a whole cuttlefish or squid or a squid/lugworm cocktail being at the top of the list. Cocktails of fresh and frozen baits are very productive for the species and other baits you can use include peeler crabs, shellfish, herring and sprats. Most lures will also catch cod on occasions.

Conger and ling: A fresh flapper of mackerel is the ideal bait for these large predators. Cut the backbone and tail out of a fresh mackerel and hook it through the chin on a 6/0. A whole mackerel, slashed in the flanks to increase the scent trail, also works well.

Pollack: The species prefers lures, but adding a strip of mackerel, squid or a large head-hooked ragworm to a lure can increase its effectiveness over some wrecks.

Tope: A fillet or whole joey mackerel is considered the best general bait for tope, but in many estuary regions a silver eel segment is superior. Tope will also take a whole live or dead mackerel fished on or just off the sea bed.

Bass: These are definitely a fan of fresh baits such as a live sandeel or joey mackerel. They will also take all manner of lures, sandeel and small mackerel patterns working best.

Flatfish: Flatties are used to scrounging around inshore and are mostly caught on worms, including slightly decaying ones. Add beads, sequins or glitter spoons to the hook snoods and allow the bait and rig to move.

Ray: Fresh mackerel is the top ray bait for most of the year, with peeler crabs deadly in summer in the estuaries. In autumn and winter fresh herring is best, but squid and Bluey will also do some damage.

Smoothhounds: Peeler crab is the major food of this predator – fresh is best but frozen – especially spider crabs – can be deadly when local supplies are low. Hermit crabs definitely catch the hounds, too.

Dogfish: For most boat anglers it's more about how to avoid this species or prevent it from taking baits aimed at other fish. There really is no answer to this problem, except to use the largest possible hooks and bait.

Whiting: Fresh yellowtail lugworms, strips of clean white frozen squid, and mackerel or herring on their own or tipped on the worms, will take these fish.

BAIT DROPPERS

Groundbaiting is not often used around the UK because of deep water, strong tides and a lack of species that come up off the sea bed to feed. However, a growing number of boat anglers are using bait droppers and several commercial models are available, whilst a few charter skippers have their own devices. One is as simple as a plastic bag full of cut-up mackerel that is lowered to the sea bed and then pulled inside out so it spills its contents. Alternatives are a sack of groundbait on the anchor, or a bait dropper incorporated into the actual rig.

Worm baits can be cocktailed with a strip of fish or squid combining scent and movement.

Groundbait is usually made up of minced or mashed oily fish. Shark anglers use frozen blocks of 'chum', adding bran which soaks up the blood and juices of the minced fish which then disperse more widely and near the surface to create a slick behind the drifting boat.

A Rubby Dubby sack hung from the side of the boat or fixed to the anchor etc can be used to attract some species to the boat.

It's a fact that artificial lures catch more anglers than fish, indeed collecting lures can be as addictive as fishing itself. However, Man's ingenuity knows no bounds and many of the modern patterns look and act in the water more like a fish than a fish. Soft plastic lures especially have taken the market by storm with their amazing array of shapes and colours.

However, a lure is only as good as the target fish's willingness to take it, and some of the crudest and most ancient efforts from the past remain the deadliest. For example, the Gummi Makk, an old-fashioned rubber eel, is little more than a length of coloured plastic tube on a hook.
But from

a fish-packed venue in Norway or Iceland the Gummi can be deadly, whereas over a regularly drifted English Channel wreck it is pretty much useless. So before you clip on any lure, give it some thought. What YOU think looks like a great lure can sometimes be a long way from what the fish are looking for or taking. Better to check with the skipper, and remember – the best lure for a given day is always the one called 'Experience'.

MULTI-LURES AND FEATHERS

The most commonly used and effective multi-lures are real or synthetic feathers fished

in strings of three to six. These represent a shoal of small bait fish and are fished sink and draw – simply lift the rod, then reel in as you lower it. This method allows you to search all depths. The originals were made from white or dyed chicken feathers, and these are still very effective for everything from mackerel to cod. However, more sophisticated lure designs, materials and tying techniques are now being developed for various fish species.

Hokkais: Hokkais have a small luminous fish head design with glitter/tinsel and feather streamers, and in the small sizes they are really deadly for mackerel and for use as baited lures. The larger ones are good for cod. This is the lure that is often favoured for use with bait, a tactic popular in Ireland. Simply bait each hook with a small sliver of squid or mackerel and fish it with a slow sink and draw, allowing time for the fish to take the bait when you get a bite.

Sabiki: These are the favourite and most deadly mini-lures and are superb for catching smaller bait fish. They are a must in the tackle box during summer, but because they are made up on light line you'll need luck on your side if you hook a big fish.

Silver tinsel: A tried and tested favourite, silver tinsel with a red whipping around the hook spade is one of the charter skipper's favourites. As these begin to fall to pieces with use, they become even more deadly!

Shrimp: Several companies produce shrimp patterns in large, standard and mini sizes, the latter being especially effective for mackerel.

Daylites: Another great favourite, these tough synthetic lures are made from a silver or white reflective material with a full-length coloured whipping on the hook shank. They are very durable, and available in small and large sizes for mackerel and cod.

Mackerel feathers and lures come in strings of up to six.

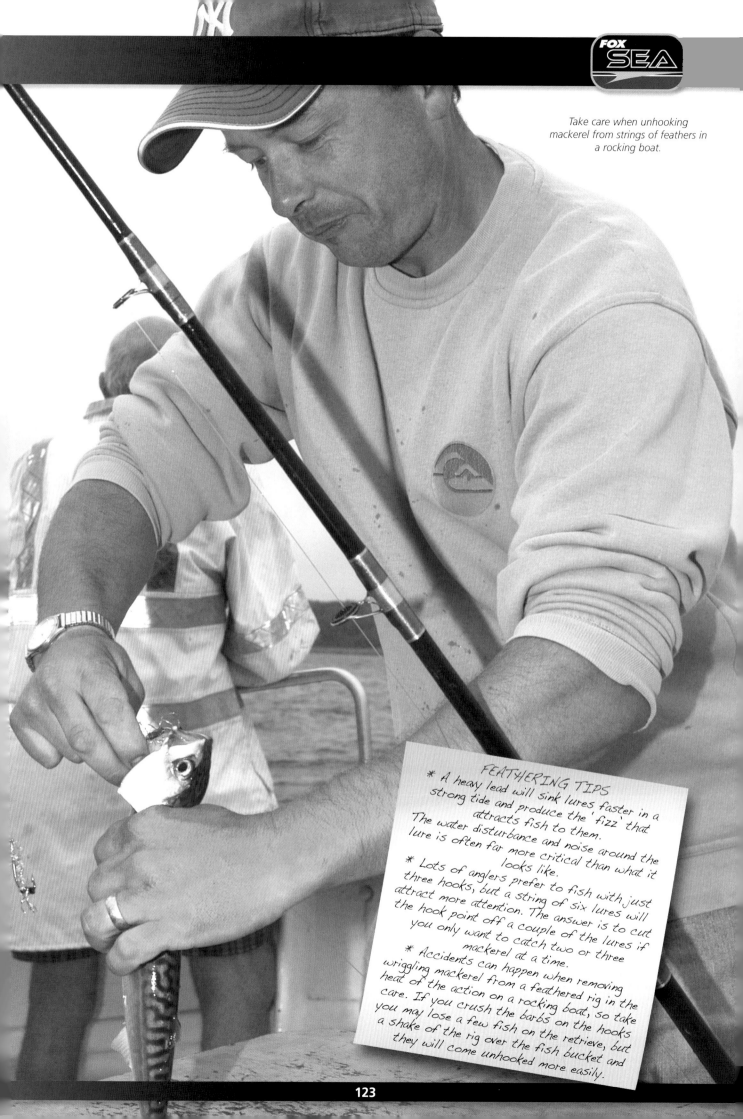

Take care when unhooking mackerel from strings of feathers in a rocking boat.

FEATHERING TIPS

* A heavy lead will sink lures faster in a strong tide and produce the 'fizz' that attracts fish to them. The water disturbance and noise around the lure is often far more critical than what it looks like.

* Lots of anglers prefer to fish with just three hooks, but a string of six lures will attract more attention. The answer is to cut the hook point off a couple of the lures if you only want to catch two or three mackerel at a time.

* Accidents can happen when removing wriggling mackerel from a feathered rig in the heat of the action on a rocking boat, so take care. If you crush the barbs on the hooks you may lose a few fish on the retrieve, but a shake of the rig over the fish bucket and they will come unhooked more easily.

Used to catch one fish at a time, lures, plugs and spinners are completely different from multi-lures and strings of feathers. Skill and finesse are required to get the best results, and fishing them is a lot more fun!

The range of lures is enormous, with a considerable cross-over between those designed for freshwater and sea fishing. Basically anything goes, and although proven designs do catch the majority of fish, there is lots of scope for experimentation.

Not a frontline boat lure, a plug is made of solid plastic or wood, and used at sea mainly for bass and for fishing close to the shore from dinghies. The most effective is the jointed, floating diver with a plastic or metal vane fixed on its nose to make it dive to a set depth. The steeper the angle and the bigger the vane, the deeper the plug dives. The Popper has a blunt or concave nose that causes it to skip and splutter across the surface, hence its name.

In all cases plugs are best fished without any additional lead. Bass, in particular, are put off by a large lead in front of a lure.

Spinners and spoons are heavier metal lures that sink quickly and can be cast further. One of the most effective for bass is the flat Dexter Wedge.

LURE FISHING TIPS

* Lures with an eye are extra effective in clear water, giving the fish something to home in on.
* Lighten down or lengthen your trace if the fish are not taking your lure. Fluorocarbon is tough, and great for long light traces for lure fishing over a wreck.
* Storing pirks can be a problem, although there are specialist bags with tubes available to keep them tidy. An old-fashioned method, still valid, is to hang the pirks by their hooks around the inside of a bucket.
* For the ultimate control and 'feel', braid line is superior to mono for lure fishing, especially with a single lure. It does, though, require a softer rod.

"Looks and action are important in a lure but lots are designed to catch anglers!"

Above: There are lots of lure options, the plastic and rubber eels etc are popular with UK boat anglers.

SHADS

Soft plastic shads are instantly recognisable. They come in various fish or shapes, and all have a lifelike wiggly tail when retrieved. Some patterns have reflective holographic colours moulded into the lure. Shads have an upward pointing hook eye to which the line is tied, and they can be fished on a long trace with a lead or, in some situations, freelined, the weight of the lure alone getting it to the sea bed.

REDGILLS AND JELLYWORMS

Redgills were the original artificial sandeel lure and remain effective, although they have been joined by a whole host of sandeel look-alikes including the softer plastic types like the Eddystone Eel and jellyworms. Soft lures are disposable and can be mounted on a jig head or a plain hook.

Jellyworms are especially effective for cod, pollack and coalfish, fished slowly as singles over wrecks and reefs on a long trace. They come in a choice of colours including luminous, natural and day-glow, and some have flame tails or twin tails.

JIG HEADS

Jig heads consist of a hook with a lead or 'head' at the eye end. This can be a realistic fish head shape or simply a ball. The secret of the lure is in the soft plastic tail that is threaded on to the hook. Available in a variety of shapes and colours, with various weights of lead and types of wiggly tail which are all interchangeable, this lure's unique movement when dropped and retrieved covers lots of species and venue situations. There are some really specialist jig heads around designed for catching specific species like cod, or even halibut.

MUPPETS

The original muppets were small plastic squid-like lures that could be slid down the hook snood above the hook. They are mainly used in conjunction with a hookbait. Cut with frilly squid-like legs, red muppets are long-standing favourites to enhance a bait. Now they are available in all colours, including luminous and

Above: A pirk on the left and Gummi Mak on the right – both excellent deep water lures for cod etc.

holographic, and in a large range of sizes. They are great for fishing the baited lure technique over a wreck or rough ground.

PIRKS

Pirks are sometimes used in conjunction with strings of lures. The original pirks were simply made from copper or stainless steel tube filled with lead, or even chromed car door handles furnished with a large treble hook. Pirks used to be stigmatised when fished amid large shoals around a wreck, amounting to nothing more than a foul-hooking device that led to lots of fish being hooked in the head, body and tail, hence their nickname 'rippers'.

Modern pirks are far more sophisticated, with single hooks to reduce foul-hooking (and snagging in the wreck) They incorporate bright holographic reflective patterns and a tough paint finish. Other changes relate to the shape of the lures and the positioning of the hook, which on many is now located on a short strong snood coming off the top of the pirk. This allows it to hang near the middle of the lure.

Pollack often prefer the sandeel shaped lures but will also take the mini pirks and fish-shaped shads.

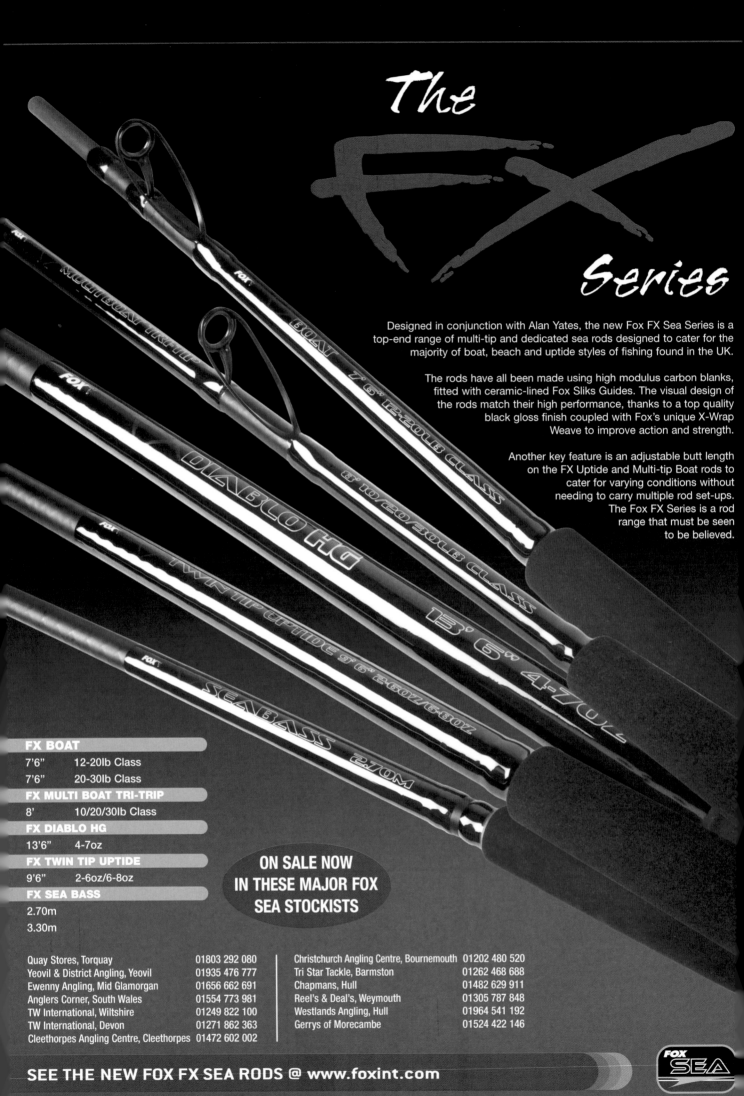

The *FX* Series

Designed in conjunction with Alan Yates, the new Fox FX Sea Series is a top-end range of multi-tip and dedicated sea rods designed to cater for the majority of boat, beach and uptide styles of fishing found in the UK.

The rods have all been made using high modulus carbon blanks, fitted with ceramic-lined Fox Sliks Guides. The visual design of the rods match their high performance, thanks to a top quality black gloss finish coupled with Fox's unique X-Wrap Weave to improve action and strength.

Another key feature is an adjustable butt length on the FX Uptide and Multi-tip Boat rods to cater for varying conditions without needing to carry multiple rod set-ups. The Fox FX Series is a rod range that must be seen to be believed.

FX BOAT
7'6"   12-20lb Class
7'6"   20-30lb Class

FX MULTI BOAT TRI-TRIP
8'   10/20/30lb Class

FX DIABLO HG
13'6"   4-7oz

FX TWIN TIP UPTIDE
9'6"   2-6oz/6-8oz

FX SEA BASS
2.70m
3.30m

ON SALE NOW IN THESE MAJOR FOX SEA STOCKISTS

SEE THE NEW FOX FX SEA RODS @ www.foxint.com

FOX SEA

Diablo® is a Registered Trademark

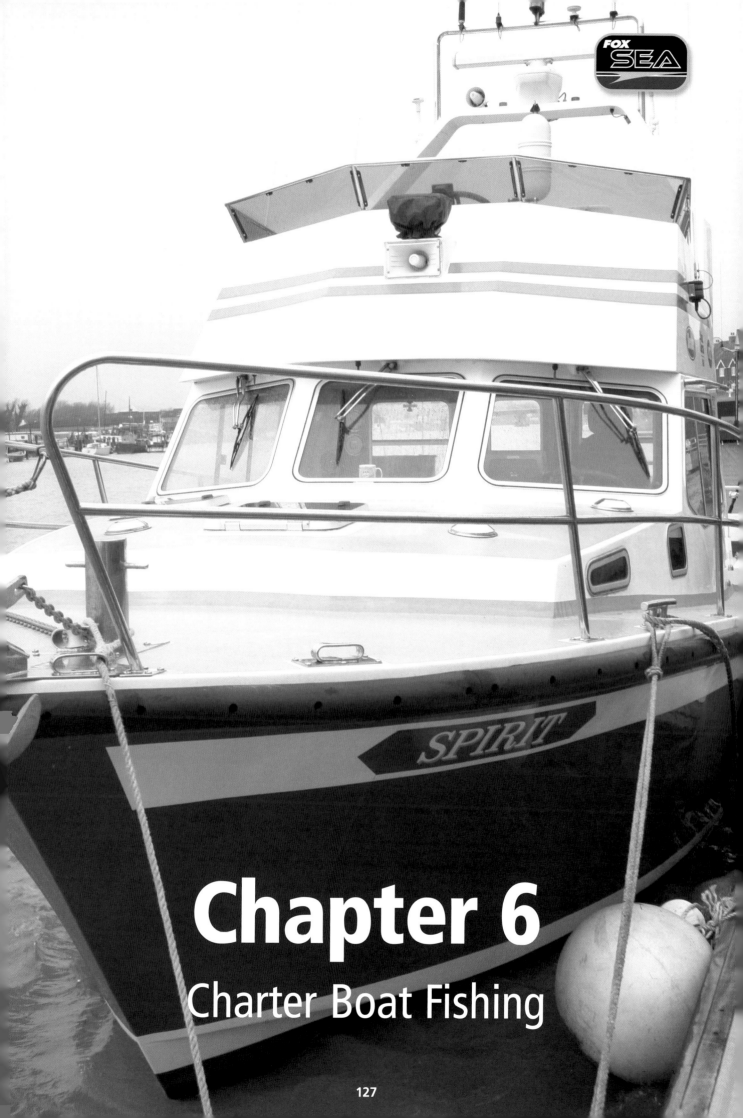

Chapter 6
Charter Boat Fishing

The charter boat gives anglers a tremendous opportunity to sample some of the best fishing around the UK. A wide range of boats are available from various ports, offering both inshore and offshore fishing, normally for between six and 12 anglers. Nowadays most angling charter boats are just that – some cater for divers as well, but few supplement their business by fishing commercially as was the case in the past, when fishing boats filled at weekends with paying anglers. Only a few charter skippers still make a bit on the side by selling the fish their anglers catch, or by netting or potting.

"Modern marinas allow charter boat access during all tides."

The professional charter skipper is out to make a profit, and this means giving customers the best possible day's fishing so that they will return. Repeat business through word of mouth keeps the best charter boats' diaries full, a sure sign of success. Trips have to be booked months, even years, in advance, and many anglers miss out on a place with a skipper who is on a roll. It might be better to try one of his rivals who fishes out of the same port

or over similar marks. Whatever your strategy, plan well ahead.

Some charter skippers are better publicity managers than others, and promote their catches with an eye to future bookings. Others, though, may let anglers catch only the fish they want via a few inaccurate drifts, and still more will use photographs from one successful session over several months of promotion and advertising.

As an angling journalist I will add that some talented skippers will catch a shedload of fish for the cameras but not offer the same treatment to 'ordinary' parties of anglers.

Most charter skippers set a price for the boat for a day's fishing, although they many also fill in days when they are not booked with individual anglers. This is particularly useful if you can be available at short notice when a

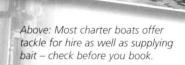

Above: Most charter boats offer tackle for hire as well as supplying bait – check before you book.

There are also boats that specialise in mackerel fishing trips around the bay, and while many an angler has cut his teeth on one of these boats, this type of party fishing is very limited in scope and is to be avoided by the serious boat angler. However, most ports nowadays have a fleet of professional charter boats, their number relating to the quality of the fishing or the customer potential.

cancellation occurs or the skipper can put together enough individual anglers to make a trip worthwhile.

TYPES OF CHARTER BOAT

Chartering once encompassed everything from trips with the local commercial fisherman part-timing between netting to the purpose-built fast charter boat designed to fish distant wrecks. In modern times charter boats have become more sophisticated, and Department of Trade and Industry regulations have ensured that boats are not only better equipped, but safer. However, there are still a number of rogue or 'cowboy' skippers who operate cheap charter trips under the guise of 'taking out their mates'. Be warned – these boats are often ill-equipped and their skippers lacking in knowledge.

The largest charter fleets, in ports and the giant modern marinas like Brighton, offer everything from inshore to offshore fishing and wrecking. In many regions, though, inshore fishing has been over-exploited and the wrecks virtually fished out. As a result, the number of bigger specialist boats that travel to distant wrecks where the fishing is better has increased in recent years, and it is these boats that attract the most customers because they continue to land the bigger fish. They are, however, also though the most expensive. A two-hour-plus journey offshore costs a lot in fuel.

Access is a big factor in attracting charter boats to a port. In many cases the smaller tidal ports have been deserted by the larger charter vessels because of the restriction the tide imposes on fishing times. It is ports with access to the sea 24/7 that are the busiest.

Most modern charter boats are large enough to accommodate up to eight anglers, and capable of fishing 20 miles-plus offshore. The DTI regulations are stiff, and all licensed boats are fully equipped with safety aids and equipment. Those specialising in long-range wrecking trips are likely to have proper flushing toilets, not the bucket in the corner of the past. Modern boats also cater for disabled anglers, and some have adopted a stern door as used by the big-game boats overseas to land giant fish. These also allow access for wheelchairs. Still other boats specialise in taking out divers to the wrecks, and a skipper with sub-aqua experience can be a big plus.

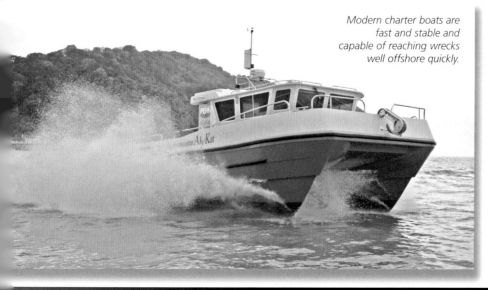

Modern charter boats are fast and stable and capable of reaching wrecks well offshore quickly.

"Clear decks ready for action!"

Choosing a charter boat is mostly common sense, but it is important to consider what you want from any trip before you book. For instance, novices may benefit from a skipper who has the patience to deal with endless questions and can supply the tackle to manage a group of inexperienced anglers. Fishing from a charter boat is not something you can learn overnight, and when several novices are on board problems can be magnified by their inexperience. So the terms 'novices welcome' and 'tackle hire/available' are worth looking out for if you or your group are new the game.

More experienced anglers may prefer a skipper who leaves them to do the fishing and simply gets on with operating the boat, although nowadays few skippers sit in the wheelhouse reading the newspaper as in the past – most are totally professional, and accept sorting their anglers as part of the job.

It's easy to be cynical about a charter skipper who baits up, strikes and does practically everything for his punters, but such skippers do exist, mainly because so many customers are not good anglers.

Skippers with a pride in their boat will take control, and over time some do treat all their customers as 'punters'. It can be most annoying for an experienced angler to be treated like an idiot. So, check out your skipper before you leave port and tell him who might need a hand and who will not.

HOW TO BOOK A CHARTER
Booking a charter boat is as simply as a telephone call or email, as long as you do it well in advance. Most reputable skippers have a website or advertisements in the national angling magazines. Avoid the part-timer or cowboy with the card in the phone box – there are still a few around despite DoT regulations.

When you book a charter boat, ask what kind of fishing is available and whether tackle is available. Does bait come with the boat price? How far out will you be fishing? Most skippers are

Check with your charter skipper the day before the trip on the type of fishing and the tackle or bait required.

happy to answer questions, but don't phone them at 10 o'clock at night or hit them with a long list of questions. Be diplomatic and friendly and you will find out what you want to know.

WEATHER PROBLEMS
The UK's weather can be so frustrating for the boat angler. Being an island, Britain is sandwiched between the Atlantic Ocean and the North Sea, both volatile stretches of windy water that greatly control and affect our weather patterns. Our predominant wind comes from the west, and is wet, while any wind from the east or north is cold. Either produces a roller coaster of gales and calm, but prolonged calm spells are rare. This means that boat angling in the open seas tends to

be spasmodic, and all skippers hope for what is termed 'a window in the weather'.

Modern boats can venture to sea in rougher weather than the past and are far safer, but fishing in any wind over a force five is uncomfortable. What's more, in the English Channel and Irish Sea there is a short uncomfortable swell as opposed to those long Atlantic rollers.

Every boat angler must learn to cope with the disappointment of a cancelled trip – it's fact of life! A crumb of comfort is that modern weather forecasting is highly accurate, although the speed of a weather front can still catch the forecasters out.

Most charter skippers will ask for a deposit, simply because the weather can often take a turn for the worse overnight and a day's trip is cancelled.

For this reason skippers will also insist on a phone call the night before a trip to run over the booking details and check on the weather. For an angler travelling long distances to a port this is a sensible thing to do. Even if there is not a full cancellation, bad weather may restrict the trip to fishing inshore and involve a change of bait, tactics and tackle. Be guided by your skipper – he wants you to catch fish and book repeat trips.

DIVER II

The best charter skippers are sponsored and offer the latest tackle.

Charter boats tend to offer some tackle for hire or free use, and now that a number of boats are sponsored by major manufacturers such as Fox, the quality of this gear can be excellent, right down to terminal rigs and accessories. Expect middle-of-the-road kit in terms of line class and weight. No skipper would want delicate tackle that could easily be ruined by the novice.

The best charter skippers are sponsored and offer the latest tackle. Navigation and fish finding electronics takes the chance out of charter fishing whilst the internet is used for weather updates, info on wrecks, recent catches etc.

For total beginners, hired tackle is the easy option because a proactive skipper will want to look after his gear and will be on hand to help. However, many anglers do prefer to use their own rod and reel, and often it's the terminal tackle that causes them more problems than anything else. Leads are heavy to carry around, and many skippers know this and carry terminal rigs and sinkers for their anglers. Always check what gear is available before you fish from a new charter boat.

Safety lines are mainly a feature of big-game or shark fishing boats, and are simply a line that is fixed between the gunnel and the reel or rod to prevent the loss of the rid should the angler let go of it etc.

THE CHARTER SKIPPER

What makes a good charter skipper? Well, in my opinion they are born that way and the handful of top skippers around the UK all have one thing in common – a sense of humour! Handling the public is bad enough, putting up with the yobbish behaviour of some sea anglers is another thing entirely. I will probably upset some people here when I say that more than

a few boat anglers are failed shore anglers who couldn't hack the demands of the shoreline and the required skills. They take to the boats for an easy life, but quickly find the skills required are basically the same, so their get-out clause is to blame the skipper for everything.

Not only that, they treat his boat like the local tip, spreading their bait and rubbish over the decks. On occasions it's worse than the Big Brother House, and some even behave as if they are at home! Small wonder many charter skippers lack a sense of humour. Becoming desensitised to cope with imbeciles is part of the job.

But now and then you come across a skipper who rises above it all and somehow seems to educate the loonies without saying much. It could be they avoid him, or that his presence attracts only the better behaved and more experienced sea anglers who appreciate his skills and his humour.

There is the other side of the coin, of course. Working for an angling magazine, I have met a few rogue skippers in my time. There are also a

large number of competent skippers still around who would benefit from a man management course. That said, the behaviour of lots of anglers is a disgrace. Small wonder many skippers can appear grumpy!

SEA SICKNESS

A common problem for charter parties is sea sickness. One angler sick can ruin the day if the boat has to return him to shore. So it's a good idea to stress to all in your group that once on board there is no return – if you come, you stay out and suffer. My advice to any angler is, if the sea is rough and you think you will be sea sick, don't go. Most know their tolerances, and often sea sickness is down purely to mind set!

Obvious ways to avoid mal-de-mer are to stay away from large amounts of alcohol the night before, get plenty of sleep and avoid a large greasy breakfast. Travel sickness pills work, and some anglers swear by wristbands. If you are vulnerable, try to get a position away from diesel fumes, avoid looking directly at the rolling waves, and drink only water and eat dry biscuits.

H aving read this far, some of you may think that charter boat fishing is easy – simply climb aboard, grab a rod and haul in the fish! But while the skipper will always be responsible for finding the fish, it's up to the angler to catch them, and that does still require a degree of angling skill.

By now you should have some idea of the different tactics, terminal rigs, baits and techniques for the various species. But aboard a charter boat you have an expert on the angling in the region on tap – the skipper – and his advice is invaluable. So many anglers, especially beginners, are stubborn in terms of taking advice once they get on a charter boat, their rush to get a hook in the water taking over their common sense. They may think they know better than the skipper, but he will have been out regularly on the same mark or wreck and will have the right tactics engraved in stone in his mind – that's not to say other methods will not work, but in all angling situations there is an easy way and a hard way!

First job on board is to find a place for your tackle. Most skippers will welcome valuables such as cameras, extra clothing and food into the cabin, but tackle should be stowed in a dry place away from spray.

Find yourself a seat. In most cases you will be welcome in the wheelhouse, but always ask the first time and don't touch ANYTHING. A chat as the boat travels to the mark can provide lots of information on how the boat and its electronics work, where the lifejackets are, the skipper's rules, and so on.

It is possible to rig rods while travelling or on arrival, but in a fast moving boat there are dangers, so this is best done before you leave the mooring.

Once over the mark, never drop your rig into the sea without the skipper's say so – he will tell you when the anchor is set or the drift is right. Similarly, when drifting, listen for the location of the wreck or reef below. Most skippers will relay this information from the wheelhouse so that tackle can be raised over the

"A tidy charter boat is a sa craft. Here boats exit a marina via the lock gates

wreck to prevent it snagging. Similarly, when asked to reel in, do it and get ready for the next drift. If you hook a fish and needs the net, call the skipper and remember, a heavy inanimate weight could be your neighbour's tackle. All parties being aware of this saves bad tangles and makes crossed lines easier to sort out.

One of the problems with a group of anglers is sorting out whose fish are who's when they are placed in the cool hold together. There are various ways around this. Skippers may mark the fish with a cut, or nick the tail or dorsal fin, but a great idea is to tag your own catch with a cable tie. That will save arguments back on the quay.

CHARTER BOAT ETIQUETTE

Treat the boat like it was your own – in other words, look after it. Small wonder many skippers will not let anglers into their wheelhouse and treat them like cattle when they cut and scatter bait on the seats, strew tackle all over the deck and – a crime that should be punishable by keel hauling – leave a lead hanging and banging the paintwork! Respect earns respect, and trust me, you will also get better fishing!

It's a fact that the stern positions in a charter boat are the hottest for fishing at anchor, because rods here are able to trot tackle back well behind the boat and away from the scare area below. Rods positioned around the

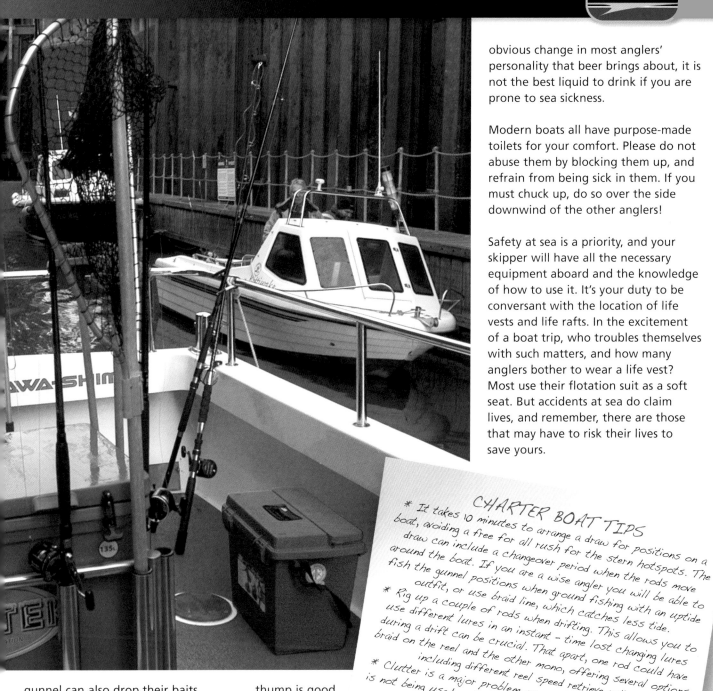

obvious change in most anglers' personality that beer brings about, it is not the best liquid to drink if you are prone to sea sickness.

Modern boats all have purpose-made toilets for your comfort. Please do not abuse them by blocking them up, and refrain from being sick in them. If you must chuck up, do so over the side downwind of the other anglers!

Safety at sea is a priority, and your skipper will have all the necessary equipment aboard and the knowledge of how to use it. It's your duty to be conversant with the location of life vests and life rafts. In the excitement of a boat trip, who troubles themselves with such matters, and how many anglers bother to wear a life vest? Most use their flotation suit as a soft seat. But accidents at sea do claim lives, and remember, there are those that may have to risk their lives to save yours.

CHARTER BOAT TIPS

* It takes 10 minutes to arrange a draw for positions on a boat, avoiding a free for all rush for the stern hotspots. The draw can include a changeover period when the rods move around the boat. If you are a wise angler you will be able to fish the gunnel positions when ground fishing with an uptide outfit, or use braid line, which catches less tide.
* Rig up a couple of rods when drifting. This allows you to use different lures in an instant – time lost changing lures during a drift can be crucial. That apart, one rod could have braid on the reel and the other mono, offering several options including different reel speed retrieve ratios.
* Clutter is a major problem on any boat, so stow gear that is not being used out of the way and don't leave anything lying around for others to trip over.
* A waterproof bag (called an overboard bag) is a great addition to your gear for stowing waterproofs on a wet day. Sea spray can get inside tackle boxes, especially cantilever trays, and heading out to sea on a rough day can see the spray lashing the deck, so check with the skipper and store valuable tackle in the dry before you leave port.

gunnel can also drop their baits back, but these invariably tangle with each other.

Braid lines have greatly improved angling enjoyment – the tide is easier to combat and bites are more positive. However, a mix of braid and mono lines can be problematic, although a partial solution is to position the mono rods in the stern and the braid along the gunnels.

Uptiding (casting) from a charter boat has its own set of rules, and I do not apologise for repeating them. A casting leader with a 30lb minimum breaking strain is essential for any boat casting. There is no need for powerful casting styles (a simple overhead

thump is good enough), but this is still dangerous in a small, crowded boat, so exercise great care. The terminal rig should always be outside the boat when casting and the caster should make sure that other anglers are aware of what he about to do. Be careful of radar masts, aerials and rigging.

Never take beer on board a charter boat. Apart from the

Catamarans are increasingly popular as charter boats because of their stability and fishing space.

Fishing is the world's largest participant sport, and no matter where you go you will find anglers and angling action. However, the UK or European style of boat angling with bait on the sea bed is not so nearly as popular worldwide as lure fishing.

"Norway offers some magnificent scenery as well as a wealth of giant fish."

NORWAY AND ICELAND

I can recommend a trip to Norway or Iceland for any boat angler who is struggling to catch a big cod. Not being members of the EU, both countries have managed their fish stocks carefully and not allowed indiscriminate fishing to damage stocks.

The Norwegians, in particular, have fish-stacked deep water fjords full of big cod, coalfish, haddock, pollack and halibut. Nets are not used by their commercial boats. Only line-caught fish may be landed, and there is even a limit on the amount of filleted fish visiting anglers can take home. This was imposed after the Germans and the Poles took the mickey by turning up in refrigerated vans.

Specialist dinghy fishing is widely available, and the boats are well equipped with navigation and fish-finders, plus the essential safety equipment. Because of the sheltered nature of the fishing, these craft are easy to handle. ➤

Above: Alan Yates with Norwegian cod.

The limited number of charter boats in Norway are mainly commercial boats that take anglers, but their catches prove the ability of the skippers. The fishing, especially in the north of the country, is spectacular both in terms of the size of the fish and the scenery. The only drawback is that the cost of living is high and fishing can be expensive.

> *"There are plenty of angling opportunities over seas, especially for giant game fish."*

All fishing here is with lures, and pirks, Gummi Makks, jellyworms, shads, Hokkais and the like are essential. My advice if you go there is to take a mix of gear, with a 12lb class braid outfit for some fun inshore fishing and a 30lb outfit for the bigger stuff. The biggest pirks and lures catch the biggest cod, and they may require a heavier outfit. Another essential is a depth counter, and some anglers favour electric reels to handle the great water depths.

One of the biggest plus points about Norway is the sheltered fishing. If you are prone to sea sickness, you can catch big cod and the like inside the shelter of the fjord. I have taken cod to over 30lb just 500 metres from the landing quay where I lodged, and it was more like fishing a lake than the open sea.

BIG-GAME

All anglers should experience fishing from a big-game boat at some time in their lives. Rods tend to be shared, which gives this type of fishing an element of luck – that is, unless you can afford to rent the boat for yourself in which case you will have access to all the rods when a fish hits.

The basic tactic is trolling lures. The boat's wake mimics a shoal of bait fish which pulls in the largest pelagic billfish predators like marlin, sailfish

Below: A blue shark out of Milford Haven aboard White Water.

and tuna. Various giant lures are trolled at different distances and depths behind the boat to attract, tease and hopefully catch the fish. It is just about the most exciting boat fishing going.

Tackle is generally supplied and the gear operated by a crew member. This is an element that some anglers may not appreciate, and results around the world are by no means guaranteed. There are also many regions of the world where you can fish for sharks, and this type of fishing offers the ultimate adrenaline rush.

Tunny are one of the most powerful of the tropical species.

Ever seen a travel rod do this?

PERMIT. 35lb
FLORIDA.

60

BLUE
MARLIN

25
KE

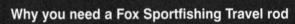

Why you need a Fox Sportfishing Travel rod

- Braid friendly Fuji guides
- Range of multiplier and fixed spool models
- 14 high quality travel rods in the initial range
- Supplied in zip top hardcases for transportation in luggage
- Unique blank compound specifically designed for multi-piece rods

IGFA
Corporate
Member

Check out the full range @ **www.foxsportfishing.com**

Chapter 7
Small Boat Fishing

Owning your own boat is every sea angler's dream – it means you can fish when and where you like, a great concept in theory. In practice a major problem is the huge amount of effort required to operate, maintain, launch, store or moor your boat. All cost time and money. The frustration of trips being cancelled because of bad weather also hampers enthusiasm and owning your own boat can be more difficult than marriage. Small wonder the majority of the nation's boat anglers prefer the easy life and fish aboard charter boats.

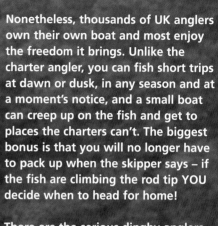

Nonetheless, thousands of UK anglers own their own boat and most enjoy the freedom it brings. Unlike the charter angler, you can fish short trips at dawn or dusk, in any season and at a moment's notice, and a small boat can creep up on the fish and get to places the charters can't. The biggest bonus is that you will no longer have to pack up when the skipper says – if the fish are climbing the rod tip YOU decide when to head for home!

There are the serious dinghy anglers who tow their craft around the coast, even over to Ireland, and there are those that belong to a local angling or boat club and operate a dinghy week in, week out from a fixed mooring or a beach ramp and slipway. Others have larger craft permanently moored in a marina or harbour.

Boat angling can be as much fun or as complicated as you want to make it, and my advice to the angler who operates his own boat is twofold and simple. First, have great respect for the sea and do not ignore the obvious dangers. Many generations of sailors have already died so that we can go afloat safely, and there is no need to take risks. Second, find a buddy – two anglers sharing a boat is not only a minimum safety arrangement, it pools knowledge, funds, common sense, tackle and the work load, and the latter is not to be ignored, especially if you tow a dinghy.

"Fast, compact, self contained and safe; the small boat angler is very well organised nowadays."

Modern small boats are fast and safe, with lots of complete packages available that will top 30mph. Fast boats offer a degree of safety in getting back inshore, although they may also confer a false sense of security.

Whatever you choose, it is essential to get the right engine for your boat and this is where the dealer comes in. An over-large engine will use excess fuel and cause the boat to ride badly in a big sea. In time it could even damage the transom. Boat and engine packages are increasingly popular, because inboard engines are more reliable than ever for the purpose-built mid-sized angling boat.

You may only want to fish when it's calm, but the weather can spring up and a rough sea can rise quickly, so you'll want a safe, stable boat that you can rely on. Plenty of room will be needed for storage, so that clutter can be stowed safely out of the way. The modern trend is away from the open dinghy towards compact and purpose-built angling boats with inboard or outboard engines. There are a variety of choices:

The centre console or 'walk around' is popular, but the position of the console does affect how the boat behaves at anchor and its suitability for angling.

Left: Modern outboards are fast and reliable.

"If you intend to tow your boat – the size and weight are important in respect to what your car can tow"

Aluminium boats are increasingly popular because of their lightness, durability and easy maintenance.

The cuddy at the bow is increasingly favoured because of the protection it gives the occupants. This design is flexible and ideal for all types of sea angling.

The enclosed cabin design is generally the largest of the small boats, with a bulkhead and cockpit bringing so many comforts to the angler – not only protection from the sea and weather, but storage space away from the action. There is potential for a cooking facility, toilet and live bait wells, and the cabin allows you to store gear aboard the boat with a degree of security.

Just one word of warning if you intend to tow your boat – the size and weight are important in respect to what your car can tow, and just as with caravans there are laws governing this subject.

Your insurance could be voided if you get this equation wrong!

A basic set of electronics is considered as essential as flares and a life jacket for the small-boat owner. Electronics relates to three main products – VHF radio, GPS (Sat Nav) unit and fish finder, although the latter two are now available in one unit. Electronic equipment updates continually. The cost has fallen dramatically in recent years, but you still get what you pay for, so be warned.

of these units and remember, they are not God, but aids to safety and better fishing. Common sense and experience remain the most reliable qualities that lead to safety and success.

I first put to sea as a junior in a clinker-built dinghy with an old Seagull outboard strapped on the stern with luggage straps. In those

days Health & Safety did not exist, and I daresay we took chances going to sea in bad weather and with inferior gear. However, I served an apprenticeship that few modern anglers experience at a time when there were plenty of fish to catch, and the dinghy angler relied on his knowledge of the region and its fish. Electronic aids, especially navigators,

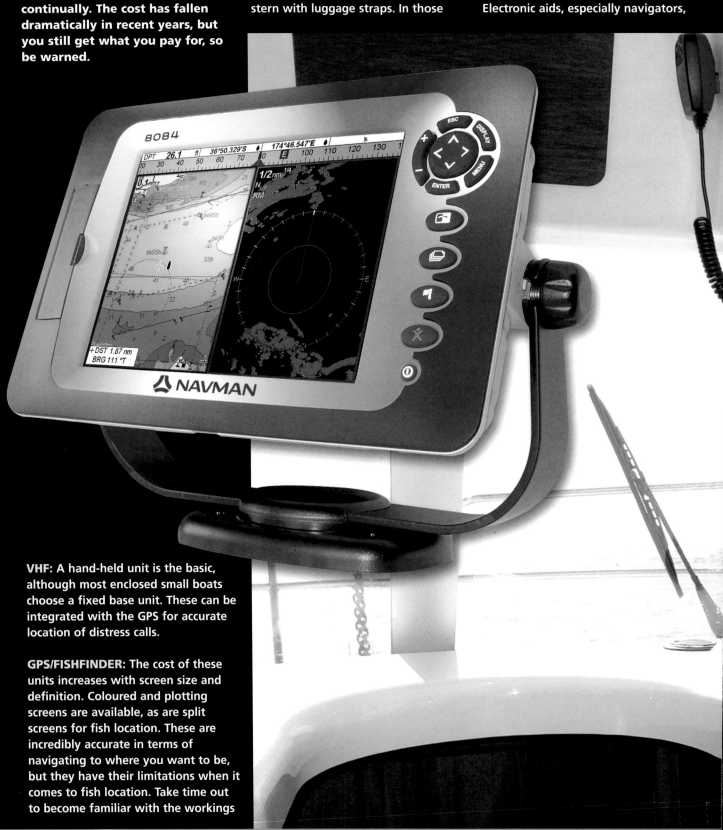

VHF: A hand-held unit is the basic, although most enclosed small boats choose a fixed base unit. These can be integrated with the GPS for accurate location of distress calls.

GPS/FISHFINDER: The cost of these units increases with screen size and definition. Coloured and plotting screens are available, as are split screens for fish location. These are incredibly accurate in terms of navigating to where you want to be, but they have their limitations when it comes to fish location. Take time out to become familiar with the workings

did not exist and it was not until the 1970s that the crudest depth-sounders came on the scene. I lined up the local pier head with a TV aerial or lighthouse and that was as technical as fish location got.

Okay, in those days there were plenty of fish, and hit-and-miss mark location often produced fish anyway!

Going out in your own boat for the very first time with limited local fishing knowledge holds the same thrills for the novice as it always did, although nowadays there are plenty of boat and seamanship courses where you can learn the safety and boat handling basics.

Below: Small fish finders and sat navs are standard for the small boat angler as well as the charter boat.

"VHF Radio is required in many ports and marinas – note the keys on a float."

TOP TIP
Look out for the RYA Powerboat courses, books, safety advice etc. Training courses are available around many parts of the UK.
Tel: 0845 3504000
Website: www.rya.org.uk

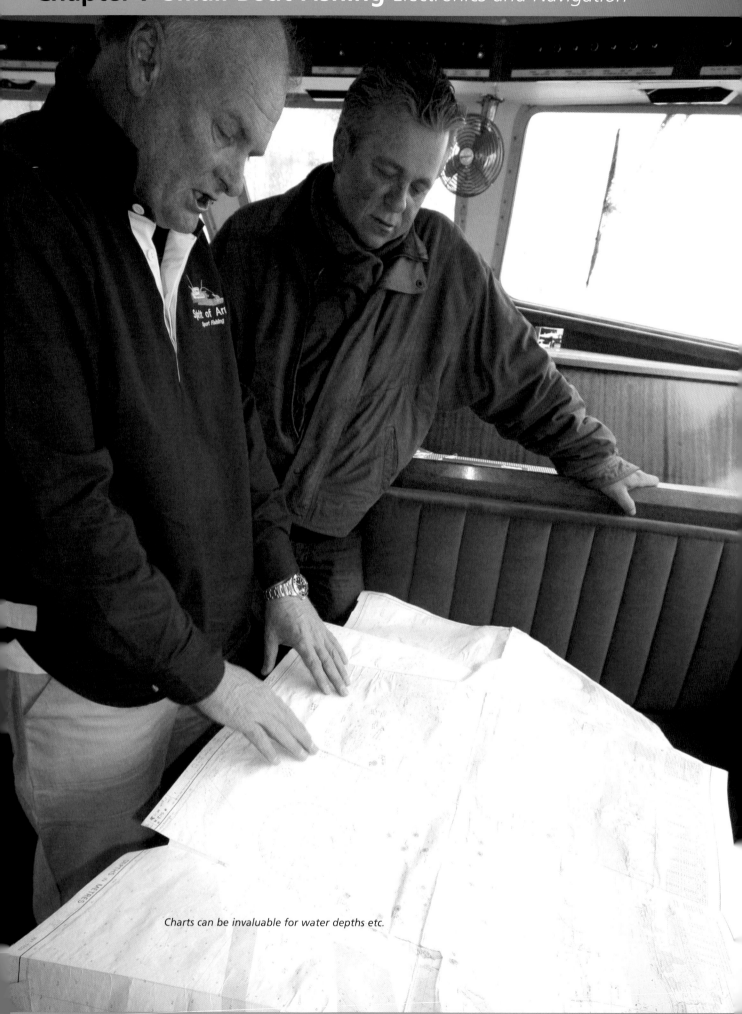

Charts can be invaluable for water depths etc.

Nowadays satellite navigation has made most car drivers as good as the professional taxi driver at finding their destination, and it's the same afloat.

The GPS and VHF radio have become essential fixtures of every boat, and even the smallest dinghy is able to know exactly where he is and have contact with the emergency services if needed. The advantages of this are tremendous, not only in terms of safety but for fishing results. It's possible to find all the marks you need and listen in on what others are catching and where.

Once logged in on the GPS you can return to the same mark time and again, and numbers play a vital part in most small-boat owners' plans. Some you will find yourself, some you will scrounge from other anglers and charts, and with time and experience you will be able to anchor or drift over the most productive parts of the sand bar, reef or wreck. Take an hour or so to learn how to navigate around your new electronics, just as you would with a new DVD or mobile telephone.

CHARTS
No small-boat owner angler should be without a chart of the region he is fishing. Apart from this being an essential for navigation (although high definition satellite plotters have made it all too easy), the chance of an electronic failure is always there, and the chart could be your only back-up. In any case, a large-scale chart can reveal lots of extra useful information including depths, sea bed features, firing ranges, tide rips, tide direction and strength, navigation buoys and even the composition of the sea bed.

"Every boat angler is an expert on navigation but common sense remains the most reliable safety instinct."

> VHF TIP
> Poor radio performance is common on small boats, the VHF cables, connections, aerial and the set-itself all vulnerable to the salt air. Don't leave it on the boat, and check the set-up regularly. A common problem is the handset transmit button jamming if it is not regularly maintained. Lots of waterproof, even floating VHF sets are available.

SMALL BOAT INFO

• Bring your own boat (BYOB) is a term that arose in boat match fishing, with towed dinghies becoming very popular in recent decades – so popular that a host of large dinghy festivals exists around the UK. Facilities for the towed dinghy can be found at most coastal locations. Tide heights can greatly affect conditions when launching from slipways, so make sure that access is not muddy over a spring tide low water.

• In the UK fibre glass dinghies are most popular, but around the world aluminium and, increasingly, the modern plastic are considered better because they are stronger and lighter. Aluminium, especially, makes for a lighter towing load. A smaller engine is required and aluminium is easy to maintain, as it welds easily.

• Three times the depth is the recommended length of anchor rope but often more (up to five times) is required in very strong tides, correspondingly less in a light tide. A length of chain attached to the anchor is essential, because it helps the anchor dig in.

Above: Fishing in pairs adds an extra element of safety.

Left: DO NOT MOOR UP TO NAVIGATION BUOYS ETC.

The current trend (some may call it a craze) is fishing from a small craft like a canoe or kayak, bringing with it an element of thrill-seeking.

Kayak fishing has also introduced the notion of stealth, especially when lure fishing for bass. A complete range of angling kayaks and specialised equipment, including dumpy rods, is available. It's not for me, though – I prefer my home comforts when I go to sea.

"Kayak fishing is not for the feint-hearted."

Above: Support the RNLI because you never know when you may need them.

Right: All safe! A life jacket is not just for kids.

SAFETY

● Fortunately lots of safety advice for first-time boat owners is available via the RYA, although it is a fact that you can go to sea without any form of test of your ability or your craft's seaworthiness – unlike on land. This is strange considering the heightened dangers.An essential for the angler is a flotation suit, although in summer these are often too warm to wear and many of the cheap models are only buoyancy aids suitable for competent swimmers in sheltered waters where help is close at hand. Look for the following specifications:
EN 393, 50N-BS, EN ISO 12402-5
A life jacket or full flotation suit is more suitable for non-swimmers in inshore waters, although they are not guaranteed to self-right an unconscious swimmer. Recommended specifications are: EN 395, 100N- BS, EN ISO 12402-4
Choose personal buoyancy that fits, and that suits the type of boating you are doing. A self-inflating vest may be suitable for angling in the summer, but a full flotation suit is more practical in winter. This correct choice ensures that you will be wearing some sort of buoyancy aid should an accident occur, rather than using your flotation suit as a soft seat!

● You can have your boat checked by the Royal National Lifeboat Institute (RNLI). It will carry out a free annual safety check of your boat for you – contact your local lifeboat station for details. A lot of the heartache in boating

is attached to the trailer or outboard. Make sure these have been serviced and checked over too.

● Inboard or outboard engines require regular maintenance. Cutting corners on servicing is asking for problems at sea. Outboards are usually serviced every 100 hours, a good reason to log your hours and ensure your engine is at least serviced before each summer season. Spare engines are now also considered a priority for emergency use.

● Before you set out to sea always check the inshore weather forecast and tides and let someone know when and where you are going and when you will return, either the local marina office or family or friends. An alternative is to register your details with the local Coastguard's safety identification scheme. Don't be afraid to turn back or cancel your trip if conditions are deteriorating.

● Sealed flare packs are ideal for the small-boat owner but can go out of date. Do not dispose of old flares in the dustbin. Check with the local police or Coastguard on the procedure.

This is not a book about how to operate a boat, it's about fishing from a boat and as such assumes a degree of seamanship and that a structurally sound vessel built to handle a rough sea is being used. However, be warned that the skills of the charter skipper that you took for granted take a long time to learn. Seamanship and angling knowledge do not happen overnight!

By far the most popular form of small-boat fishing is from the inshore dinghy in shallow water. The freedom to fish when and where you want, with as many rods as you wish, takes some beating, and if you are not catching you can always up anchor and move to another spot. The privacy and personal comfort of small-boat fishing is what draws many to it, but the downside may be that you don't have the charter skipper to fall back on when a problem arises. This is why I have included a small section on some of the basic tactics and problems of operating a small boat.

ANCHORING

A good anchor is essential. There are various designs, some for a particular type of sea bed, others for all-round fishing, and opinions differ on what is best. You will need at least four times the depth of anchor rope, and 12ft of chain is standard to help the anchor to set.

In general the anchor should be fixed so that it can be 'tripped' – this involves securing the chain at the sharp end of the anchor and then tying it to the main shackle at the top with a weak link such as string – lots of anglers now use a cable tie. If you get stuck, the plastic tie breaks and you haul the anchor in upside down.

Accurate anchoring comes with practice because the tide, wind and your timing or skill all affect where you eventually end up. With GPS, anglers can become paranoid about not being exactly in the right spot, although hauling the anchor is a deterrent to having several tries. It's best to get it right first time.

Easy, safe access to the bow for anchoring.

Cable ties are ideal for tripping an anchor.

WEATHER AND PROBLEMS

Wind and tide are forever changing, and the small-dinghy angler can be put at risk should the weather worsen. Obviously I would expect anglers to check the weather before leaving port, especially with a mind to the likely conditions when they want to return. Wind with tide usually produces a calm sea, but wind against tide generates rougher conditions. When you have a stiff breeze against a large powerful spring tide, steep waves appear rapidly, so check wind directions, force and tide times and heights before you decide where you are going to fish.

Fortunately, GPS has helped to ease the problems caused by mist and fog, but a small boat is at risk because it may be too small to be picked up by a larger vessel's radar. Keep your wits about you and your eyes and ears open, and don't travel flat out.

Today's engines are very reliable, but they can still fail – a good reason to fish with other boats and to carry a spare 'get you home' engine. The rule is always to start the engine before you pull the anchor, or, if you experience engine failure while travelling, to drop the anchor. Drifting is not a good idea because it will make it more difficult for rescuers to find you.

"When in doubt always take the safe option."

Above: Slipway access is important to the small boat angler but check on access throughout the tide range.

LAUNCHING

Launching a trailed small boat down a slipway poses few problems, although lots of slips don't extend to the low water mark. That makes them tide restricted, and that can pose problems launching or landing. Those that are accessible on all tides are popular, but that in turn may lead to problems with car and trailer parking. That's why lots of small-boat owners join a club and many around the coast have their own landing winch, parking and trailer compound and clubhouse.

There is a saying about many hands making light work, and fishing in a club situation has many attractions, not least of these being its many volunteers.

SMALL-BOAT FISHING

Tackle and tactics are basically as in the previous chapters, although gear can be more refined, and personalised to suit your boat or the region you fish. For instance, you don't have other anglers to worry about so two anglers can use and mix very light tackle, fish with braid or use uptide tactics without fear of tangles.

BAITING THE HOOK

This would seem a simple task, but it is an area where many boat anglers fail. In their haste to get a bait into the water they present it so badly that fish either remove it without being hooked, or the bait slips down the hook shank and blocks the point.

Rule one is that the hook size should match the bait, rule two is that the bait should be presented to give you the best chance of hooking the fish. Remember, dropping a bait to the sea bed can destroy its presentation! Finally, regularly replace your hookbait with fresh. Scent and juices are essential to attract fish to your offering, and continuing fishing with a washed-out bait is doomed to failure.

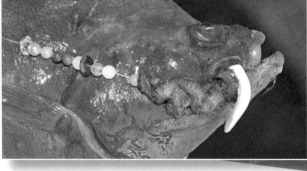

Above: Beads and sequins enhance bait presentation.

Lugworms: For the smaller species (whiting, codling, dabs) thread the hook (a 1/0 Aberdeen is a good all-round size) through the worm, head or tail first – it's your choice – without leaving ends and loops sticking out for the fish to grab. For multiple worm baits slid up the hook snood use a Pennell hook sliding on the snood, so that there is a hook at either end of the bait. Lots of small lugworm baits can have just as much scent as a single large one, and multi-baits do set up a feeding frenzy among the small species, which in turn attract bigger fish.

TACKLE TIP
The most effective terminal rig for bottom fishing from a small boat is a spreader, because it presents baits close to the sea bed. Metal is often replaced by plastic, but some say metal booms are superior because they create a magnetic field, and the noise they make attracts fish.

"Fish welfare from a small boat – here a tope is returned."

Ragworms: Fished in small bunches, the wriggling tails attract lots of the small species, while a whole large ragworm is an excellent bait for some of the larger predators.

Squid: The smaller Calamari squid make an excellent big-fish bait and can be mounted on a Pennell rig or fished in strips tipped on to lugworm.

Mackerel: This is the best all-round bait from the small boat, especially in summer, fished in large fillets on a Pennell rig for the large species or as strips on their own or tipped with worm.

Cocktail: The most effective baits are cocktails of two or more baits and there are no rules – mix anything to hand or that takes your fancy.

BITE DETECTION AND STRIKING

Relax and watch your rod tip from a dinghy in a calm sea and you will spot even the most delicate flatfish bite. In a heavy sea, however, the movement of the rod tip and end tackle on the sea bed in tide can be as much as 6ft, and even the strongest bites can be hard to determine. Braid line has made bite spotting easier, but braid used in a heavy sea has its own problems because it exaggerates any movement, including that of sea and tide, and from a small boat that can mean the bait is moved dramatically on the sea bed.

Typical of the many problems of the sea angler, the cure is a compromise. Switch to mono line which has lots of stretch, and therefore soaks up the movement or, if using braid, add a mono leader to the end. Generally the answer to bite spotting in a rough sea or a heavy swell is to increase the length of line between rod tip and end

tackle, either by casting out from the boat or letting the tackle trot back in the tide.

But when you see a bite, when do you strike, how hard, and do you need to strike more than once? Personally I feel that striking is overrated, but many anglers cannot fish without reacting to a tapping rod tip. If a rod bends over the gunnel, the fish is usually hooked anyway. If there is one rule, it is to allow fish time to take the bait, although if you want to return what you catch alive there is a case for striking as soon as possible.

It is all down to the angler. Some only strike at hard bites, some strike at every single twitch of the rod tip, others don't strike at all, merely retrieve at set intervals.

Double striking is a tactic used for sharks, including tope, and with heavy gear for very big game fish with tough

bony jaws. Don't strike too hard if you are fishing light – just lifting into a fish is usually sufficient to set the hook.

Your results will eventually tell you when and what is the best way to strike, although if you want the ultimate precision experience nothing beats holding the rod and feeling the bites through your fingers.

> **MISSED BITE TIP**
> Lengthen your hook snoods if you are missing bites. This allows the fish more room to take the bait without moving the lead or rod tip, and may even give the fish more confidence. If that does not work, give the bite more time.

Fishing uptide bites are registered as a slack line as the fish pulls the grip lead from the sea bed.

BAIT AND CATCH WELFARE

Within the confines of a small boat, bait and catch storage is paramount. Anything left scattered around the deck poses safety issues.

Some would say that bait is most important, and indeed it is wise not to get all your bait out at once in sun,

"Forceps can be used for hook removal"

wind or rain. Keep some back for later and remember, bait kept in tip-top condition can be used another time. A small cool box or bag is especially useful for bait for most of the year, while a large open-mouth food flask is ideal for storing frozen baits like sandeels, squid and mackerel fillets out of the hot sun.

Most anglers use a large fish box for their catch although increasingly the modern lidded cool boxes offer a more secure, compact and cool place for the catch and the bait.

Fish keep best when gutted immediately after capture. Left in a pile, even in a cool box, fish flesh against fish flesh softens up. Filleting on board is the best way there is to preserve fish, and the bonus is that there are no smelly heads and offal to dispose of at home!

CATCH AND RELEASE

Catch and release is increasingly popular among small-boat anglers, simply because you can make choices. Aboard a charter boat the skipper often snaffles your catch before it hits the deck, but in

your own boat you can chose to return what you want. Most anglers are now realising that the smaller fish taste best, while the bigger breeding fish are most valuable in maintaining fish stocks. Increasingly, small-boat competitions are run along catch and release lines with points for the species, weight for length, or simply specimen fish.

Above: The T Bar disgorger is a favoured tool for removing big hooks from big toothy critters.

UNHOOKING

Unhooking fish is a major problem for the novice angler, and a disgorger like a T bar or similar takes some getting used to. With practice

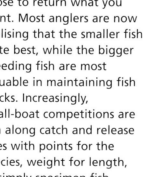

Left: Take care of your bait supply – don't leave it all out in the sun and spray.

hooks can be removed safety and fish returned alive, but the angler needs to accept that hooking a fish in the mouth can sometimes be fatal. Although cutting the line and leaving the hook in is an option, it is rarely the solution. If you want to practise conservation, look closely at your chosen hook size – small hooks do the least damage and are easier to remove. Barbless hooks are another option, and although they are not generally available for sea angling, crushing the barb with pliers is a practical compromise.

Chapter 8
More on Wind and Weather

WIND AND TERMS

WIND DIRECTION:
Indicates the direction the wind is blowing FROM

BECOMING CYCLONIC:
Indicates that there will be a considerable change in wind direction across the path of a depression within the forecast area

VEERING:
A change of wind direction clockwise, such as south-west to west

BACKING:
A change of wind anticlockwise, such as south-east to north-east

SEA STATES

SMOOTH:
Wave height less than 0.5m

SLIGHT:
Wave height of 0.5m to 1.25m

MODERATE:
Wave height of 1.25m to 2.5m

ROUGH:
Wave height of 2.5m to 4m

VERY ROUGH:
Wave height of 4m to 6m

HIGH:
Wave height of 6m to 9m

VERY HIGH:
Wave height of 9m to 14m

PHENOMENAL:
Wave height more than 14m

FORECAST ARRIVAL TIMES

IMMINENT:
Expected within six hours

SOON:
Expected in six to 12 hours

LATER:
Expected in more than 12 hours

VISIBILITY

VERY POOR:
Visibility less than 1,000m

POOR:
Visibility between 1,000m and two nautical miles

MODERATE:
Visibility between two and five nautical miles

GOOD:
Visibility more than five nautical miles

The weather, particularly wind direction and strength, can have a dramatic effect on the sea, and nothing brings that home more painfully than a gale that stops boats getting out.

Put simply, Earth's weather is in the lowest six miles of the air we breathe, and above this it is always still. That's why jet aircraft fly above this layer, which is known as the troposphere. The water drawn up from the sea in this lowest layer of the atmosphere produces the constant swirling and stirring that we call the weather.

Winds are caused by the heat of the sun warming up the land, sea and air.

consider wind direction or strength, especially localised sea breezes produced by the lower air temperature over wide expanses of ocean. One thing you need to know is that wind speed and strength over a flat sea is far different to that over land. Add in the fact that the sea rises and falls up to 50ft, and that tidal movement against a wind also has a big influence on wind speed and timing, and you realise just what the forecasters are not telling you!

For small-boat owners, the most reliable information is available from the *Inshore Waters* or the *National Shipping Forecasts* – **www.bbc.co.uk/weather/coast/shipping**

Above: The Marina may be calm but outside in the open sea conditions will be different.

Cold air is sucked in under rising warm air and the turning of the Earth from west to east spins the winds flowing between the equator and the poles.

You can determine wind direction and strength by looking at a wind vane, or even holding up a wet finger, but a more accurate forecast of wind direction and strength is essential before you go to sea in a boat.

The TV weather forecast is not reliable enough because the pretty but sometimes dippy female presenters are only programmed to talk about sunshine and rain. Few mention or

The Inshore Waters forecast is favoured because the *National forecast* is for 24 hours, and often the weather threatened may not be arriving for 12 hours-plus, but it acts as a fail-safe for anglers travelling well offshore or those in doubt about setting out.

There may be alternatives when the wind is strong, and some would say a sheltered inshore trip is better than no trip at all. On thing for sure, do not go to sea or take risks when the weather is against you. Modern sea weather forecasts are so accurate there is just no way you should chance it.

MAP OF SEA AREAS

SE Iceland

Faeroes

Bailey

Fair Isle

Viking

N.Utsire

Hebrides

Cromarty

S.Utsire

Rockall

Malin

Forties

Forth

Fisher

Tyne

Dogger

German Bight

Shannon

Irish Sea

Humber

Fastnet

Lundy

Thames

Dover

Sole

Portland

Wight

Plymouth

FitzRoy

Biscay

Traflgar

BEAUFORT SCALE

The Beaufort scale is used to show the wind force and its effect on the sea's surface. Of course, wind direction has a great effect on the sea's roughness, and an offshore wind can produce very calm conditions close to shore. In general any wind over a force six that is onshore produces difficult conditions to go to sea in a small boat.

Beaufort Scale	Wind Speed	Description	State of Sea	Wave height
0	0 to 1 knots	Calm	Like a mirror	–
1	1 to 2	Light Air	Slight ripple	4ins
2	2 to 5	Light Breeze	Small wavelets	7ins
3	5 to 9	Gentle Breeze	Large wavelet/crests	2ft
4	13	Mod Breeze	Small wave/crests	3ft
5	19	Fresh Breeze	Mod waves/spray	6ft
6	24	Strong Breeze	Large wave/foam/spray	9ft-10ft
7	30	Near Gale	Sea heaps/foam/blown	13ft
8	37	Gale	Mod high waves	18ft
9	41	Severe Gale	High waves	–
10	48	Storm	–	–
11	56	Violent storm	–	–
12	64	Hurricane force*	–	–

*Not usually experienced in UK

The old saying *'when the wind is in the east the fish bite least'* is considered very true by lots of sea anglers, although it does depend on what UK coast you are on. The reputation of east winds in some coastal regions relates to late winter, when few fish are around anyway, but enough evidence exists to suggest that an east wind and a low-pressure area together affect fish behaviour. Such knowledge can enable the sea angler to fish at the best times, avoiding the most unproductive conditions.

The other old sayings generally ring true. *'When the wind blows west the fish bite best'*: Definitely the case more often than not.

'When the wind blows south the bait falls in the fishes' mouth': Again, spot-on.

'When the wind blows north the fish bite for all they are worth': Not so sure about this one, although a north wind can be productive, depending on where you are.

In the past those living near the sea hung out strands of kelp, a seaweed which in dry weather shrivels and is dry to the touch. If rain threatens it swells and becomes damp.

Anglers will hear many other old wives tales and superstitions relating to fishing. Most have a ring of truth to them and should not be dismissed. One that I set much store by is *'red sky at night,*

shepherd's delight' – so often the red sky signals a beautiful day ahead. *'Red sky in the morning, shepherd's warning'* spells trouble, because nine times out of ten it signals a blustery, windswept, wet or stormy day ahead.

Many sea anglers, including charter skippers, set store by superstitions handed down through generations – oddly, the same ones are current from Lands End to John O'Groats and there are certain things you just do not do on the boat of a skipper who believes in these things.

Whistling is a major no-no on some boats, on others it just annoys people. The phrase *'whistling up the wind'* harks back to the time when witches were burnt at the stake, so button those lips.

Another peculiar superstition is never to sit on an upturned bucket – don't ask me why, but I know skippers who will turn around and go straight back to port if you do.

Perhaps the oddest superstition is one I adhere to, and that is not to talk about those long-eared, fluffy-tailed animals that hop around the land and aren't hares! For many generations of seagoing folk this is a word that spells disaster, and it should be avoided. Alternative names come from around the UK such as Bexhill Donkey (Ponkoid is mine), Long Tail and Bunny. Pigs, elephants or monkeys are also taboo – *'grunter'* is a common

alternative term for the pig – while some old fishermen would not go to sea if they passed a nun, a rook or a cat on the way to their boat.

Clergy (known as *'sky-pilots'*) are generally not welcome on boats. And another superstition that might get you returned to the shore on some charter boats is stirring your tea with a knife or fork.

Left: Lots of big fish escape at the last moment so take extra care and look out for that last gasp lunge at the net.

"The size of your individual catch can be affected by luck. Can you keep a smile when lady luck is against you?"

LUCK

There are anglers who believe fishing is all about luck – granted, we all consider those that are successful as lucky and our own bad results as unlucky. Angling is strewn with chance. After all, a dumb fish is involved and they really are unpredictable.

The angler who thinks he knows it all will soon discover that he doesn't when fate or luck takes take a hand. You can, to a degree, make your own good fortune and lots of the most successful sea anglers have

a confidence and skill level that so often sidesteps luck, but even they can experience a loss of form that can spiral into one disaster after another.

You have to smile sometimes. Fate conspires against you when the Man Upstairs is turning the switches, but at the same time the joy of getting it right is something only an angler can truly appreciate, and catching the biggest fish or winning the big match is what most of us are in it for. In match fishing, seeing the

England flag going up the middle pole is an experience I will always cherish. Running it close was seeing the German flag going up the second-placed pole!

Lady Luck has served me up her fair share of disasters – a record-breaking bass that jumped the hook and the net, an engine failure that prevented a championship-winning catch reaching the scales, and a 100lb-plus conger that I fought to the gaff only to find it was also attached to the rig of a seasick angler asleep in the cabin!

Where do I start? Match fishing being dear to my heart, I have left this topic until the final chapter because it is generally a progression of learned skills that leads the freelance angler to compete formally against others. Catching fish when the angler dictates the terms is fairly straightforward – I would compare it to kicking a football – but being able to play 'keepy uppy' is another thing entirely, and the most expensive boots won't make you an England player.

The few major boat events around the UK are either charter or small-boat competitions, sometimes a mixture of both. The ambition of the skilled boat match angler, though, is to fish for his or her country, and that will be exclusively from charter boats. Finding the fish is more down to the skipper than the anglers, and winning your boat is more important than individual accolades.

Unfortunately, international boat fishing is limited to Europe because

lengths has promoted more finesse in boat angling, while the influence of Continental and worldwide tactics and gear is changing UK boat fishing.

Quiver tip rods (the tip can be changed to suit weather, tide strength and species) are now standard kit, and because catch and release is more common, lighter tackle and small hooks are used to target smaller fish. That's not to say that the larger fish are ignored, rather that Europe-based boat matchmen have found a way to be more conservation-minded by targeting the smaller, less threatened species.

The pouting or whiting 'snatch match' system is now a thing of the past, and rightly so. The weighing-in of countless dead fish which nobody wanted to eat was a serious blot on angling. Instead, a points system for species or a simple length-for-weight calculation is used.

In other events a catch limit of species is imposed, so it's fair to say that match fishing skills have become more refined in recent times.

As for the match fishing techniques, I particularly like a method called 'bottom bouncing' that is used by the Americans for flatfish. A light spinning-style rod is used with micro braid line, and bait and lures are continually flipped with the aid of the light rod tip. Similar tactics are growing in popularity off Norway for catching big halibut with lures (although the rods are substantially more beefy), while French anglers fishing Biscay are using similar light braid tactics with single-handed spinning rod to catch bass.

Match fishing never stands still, and there will always be someone willing to go a step further to win. Forget the bit about just wanting to compete, winning is what it's all about and that depends on how hard you are prepared to try.

That said, all forms of losing are the best possible training for life's winners.

Good luck!
Alan

Above: The boat matchman's first challenge is to win the boat.

Match fishing is really all about having the ability to learn from your experiences, which is why I cannot pass on any magic formula for success. The previous chapters should, though, have given you a basic idea of what's involved in sea angling from a boat.

The successful match angler prepares well and is able to think on his feet. He will be able to adapt to conditions as he finds them, and change tactics as the situation demands. The rewards from match fishing are small – no fortunes to be made, only short-lived glory and maybe a reputation for being hard to beat.

around the rest of the world game-fishing styles are the norm. If you are into that, it is possible to fish for the home nations in such world events.

In my opinions, game-fishing has little to do with skill. It's a bit like show jumping – much depends upon the boat (horse), and the fatness of your wallet. Worse still, on occasions you only get to share a rod and when it's not your turn someone can catch the winning fish – farcical!

BOAT MATCH TACTICS
The relatively recent arrival of braid main lines and fluorocarbon hook

Bass, Cod, Pout, Scad, Gurnard, Mullet

Size cms	18	19	20	21	22	23	24	25	26	27	28	29	30	31	32	33	34	35	36	37	38	39	40	41	
	8	9	10	11	12	13	14	16	18	20	22	25	28	31	34	37	40	43	47	51	55	59	63	68	
Size cms	42	43	44	45	46	47	48	49	50	51	52	53	54	55	56	57	58	59	60	61	62	63	64	65	Fish over 65 Add 15 per cm
	74	80	86	92	98	104	110	116	122	129	136	143	150	158	166	174	182	190	200	210	220	232	244	260	

Dab, Plaice, Flounder, Sole, Brill, Turbot

BRILL/TURBOT OVER 30cm = DOUBLE POINTS

Size cms	18	19	20	21	22	23	24	25	26	27	28	29	30	31	32	33	34	35	36	37	38	39	40	41	
	5	6	7	8	10	12	14	16	18	21	24	28	32	36	40	44	48	52	56	60	64	68	74	80	
Size cms	42	43	44	45	46	47	48	49	50	51	52	53	54	55	56	57	58	59	60	61	62	63	64	65	Fish over 65 Add 15 per cm
	88	100	112	124	136	148	160	172	184	196	208	220	232	244	256	268	280	292	304	316	331	346	361	375	

All Rays (Across wings)

STINGRAY = DOUBLE POINTS

Size cms	18	19	20	21	22	23	24	25	26	27	28	29	30	31	32	33	34	35	36	37	38	39	40	41	
	7	8	9	10	12	14	16	18	20	22	24	26	29	32	37	44	51	58	68	78	88	98	108	118	
Size cms	42	43	44	45	46	47	48	49	50	51	52	53	54	55	56	57	58	59	60	61	62	63	64	65	Fish over 65 Add 20 per cm
	128	140	155	170	185	200	215	230	245	260	275	290	305	320	335	350	365	380	395	415	435	455	475	500	

Whiting, Rockling, Unspecified, Poor Cod, Pollack, Coalfish

Size cms	18	19	20	21	22	23	24	25	26	27	28	29	30	31	32	33	34	35	36	37	38	39	40	41	
	5	6	7	8	9	10	11	12	13	14	16	18	20	22	24	26	28	31	34	37	40	44	48	52	
Size cms	42	43	44	45	46	47	48	49	50	51	52	53	54	55	56	57	58	59	60	61	62	63	64	65	Fish over 65 Add 15 per cm
	56	60	64	68	72	77	82	88	94	100	106	112	120	128	136	144	152	160	170	180	190	200	212	225	

Bream, Red Mullet, Wrasse

Size cms	18	19	20	21	22	23	24	25	26	27	28	29	30	31	32	33	34	35	36	37	38	39	40	41	
	8	10	12	14	16	18	21	24	27	30	33	36	40	45	50	55	60	65	70	75	80	85	90	95	
Size cms	42	43	44	45	46	47	48	49	50	51	52	53	54	55	56	57	58	59	60	61	62	63	64	65	Fish over 65 Add 10 per cm
	100	105	110	115	120	125	133	141	149	157	165	173	181	189	197	205	213	221	231	241	251	261	271	280	

All Dogfish & Smoothhound

Size cms	18	19	20	21	22	23	24	25	26	27	28	29	30	31	32	33	34	35	36	37	38	39	40	41	
	3	4	5	6	7	8	9	10	11	12	13	14	15	16	17	18	19	20	21	22	23	24	25	26	
Size cms	42	43	44	45	46	47	48	49	50	51	52	53	54	55	56	57	58	59	60	61	62	63	64	65	
	27	28	30	32	35	38	41	44	47	50	53	56	59	62	66	70	74	79	84	89	94	100	106	112	
	66	67	68	69	70	71	72	73	74	75	76	77	78	79	80	81	82	83	84	85	86	87	88	89	
	119	126	134	144	154	164	174	184	194	204	214	224	234	244	254	264	278	292	306	320	334	348	362	377	
	90	91	92	93	94	95	96	97	98	99	100	101	102	103	104	105	106	107	108	109	110	111	112	113	Fish over 113 Add 20 per cm
	392	407	422	437	452	467	482	497	512	527	544	561	578	595	612	629	646	663	680	697	714	731	748	770	

Garfish

Size cms	35	36	37	38	39	40	41	42	43	44	45	46	47	48	49	50	51	52	53	54	55	56	
	8	9	10	11	12	13	14	15	16	17	18	19	20	21	22	23	24	25	26	27	28	29	
Size cms	57	58	59	60	61	62	63	64	65	66	67	68	69	70	71	72	73	74	75	76	77	78	
	30	31	32	33	34	36	38	40	42	44	46	48	50	52	54	56	58	60	62	64	66	68	
	79	80	81	82	83	84	85	86	87	88	89	90	91	92	93	94	95	96	97	98	99	100	Fish over 100 Add 5 per cm
	70	73	76	79	82	85	88	91	94	97	100	104	108	112	116	120	124	128	132	136	140	145	

Eels

Size cms	18	19	20	21	22	23	24	25	26	27	28	29	30	31	32	33	34	35	36	37	38	39	40	41	
	1	2	3	4	5	6	7	8	9	10	11	12	13	14	15	16	17	18	19	20	21	22	23	24	
Size cms	42	43	44	45	46	47	48	49	50	51	52	53	54	55	56	57	58	59	60	61	62	63	64	65	Fish over 65 Add 2 per cm
	25	26	27	28	29	30	31	32	33	34	35	36	37	38	39	40	41	42	43	44	45	46	47	50	

Congers

Size cms	18-20	21-23	24-26	27-29	30-32	33-35	36-38	39-41	42-44	45-47	48-50	51-53	54-56	57-59	60-62	63-65	66-68	69-71	72-74	75-77	78-80	81-83	84-86	87-89	
	15	17	20	23	26	29	33	37	41	45	50	55	60	70	80	90	100	120	150	180	210	240	270	300	
	90-92	93-95	96-98	99-101	102-104	105-107	108-110	111-113	114-116	117-119	120-122	123-125	126-128	129-131	132-134	135-137	138-140	141-143	144-146	147-149	150-152	153-155	156-158	159-161	Fish over 161 Add 50 per cm
	330	360	400	450	500	550	600	650	700	750	800	860	920	980	1040	1110	1180	1250	1320	1390	1460	1530	1610	1700	

<u>Rules for measure and release</u>

1. All fish to be rounded down to the nearest cm, all fish over 18cm count.
2. Fish must be placed in a bucket of sea water and taken to the adjacent angler to be measured, witnessed and recorded on your match card, the fish must then be gently returned to the sea **immediately, in front of that angler**. Fish for the table must be dispatched and have their tail removed at this point.
3. Fish length, weight and running total, must be recorded and signed by the adjacent angler, before the next cast is retrieved.
4. Match cards must be signed off, total weight recorded and witnessed by the adjacent angler.
5. All anglers are stewards. It is in yours and everyones interest to see that correct procedures are adhered to, to ensure fair play.
5. Damaged and unreadable cards may be disqualified.
6. Weavers, mackerel, sea trout, salmon and all shads are banned.
7. Failure to comply with any of the above, or any match rules, may lead to disqualification.
<u>Fish longer than the stated chart will be awarded points marked in red for every additional centimetre.</u>

<u>Full SAMF rules over</u>

Index

Index